T0300122

The Mediterranean Welfare Regime and the Economic Crisis

This book examines the recent evolution of the Mediterranean Welfare regime, and how the economic crisis may be contributing to redefine its basic traits. Moving from the macro comparative analysis of long-term socio-demographic trends to the study of specific welfare programs, the chapters included in this book employ a variety of methods and approaches to review the specificities of the Mediterranean Welfare model. All chapters aim to analyze the role that the recent transformations experienced by Southern European societies (ageing, increasing women labour market participation, decreasing expectations for care within the family, immigration) have had over this model. The basic characteristics of this regime type are supposed to be strongly grounded in the values shared by these societies (familistic tendencies, clientelism, lack of generalized trust), but the modernization which these countries experienced in recent years contributed, with a different speed and to a different degree, to a significant transformation in their axiological foundations. The impact of the current fiscal and economic crisis on the Mediterranean Welfare regimes may be contributing to the growing de-legitimatisation of political systems of these countries, something particularly important in a region that established democratic regimes only (relatively) recently.

This book was originally published as a special issue of *European Societies*.

Francisco Javier Moreno-Fuentes is a Research Fellow at CSIC and holds a BA in Sociology (UCM), a Masters in Social Sciences (Juan March Institute, Spain), an MSc in Social Policy (LSE, UK), and a PhD in Political Science (UAM, Spain). His research focuses on the comparative analysis of public policies in different areas such as immigration, welfare regimes, and urban policies.

Pau Marí-Klose is Assistant Professor at the University of Zaragoza, Spain and holds a BA in History (UB), a Masters in Social Sciences (Juan March Institute, Spain), an MA in Sociology (University of Chicago, USA), and a PhD in Sociology (UAM). His main interests lie in the study of inequalities and social policies in areas such as child poverty, education, and intergenerational relations.

The Mediterranean Welfare Regime and the Economic Crisis

Edited by
Francisco Javier Moreno-Fuentes and Pau Marí-Klose

LONDON AND NEW YORK

First published 2015
by Routledge
2 Park Square, Milton Park, Abingdon, Oxon, OX14 4RN, UK

and by Routledge
711 Third Avenue, New York, NY 10017, USA

Routledge is an imprint of the Taylor & Francis Group, an informa business

British Library Cataloguing in Publication Data
A catalogue record for this book is available from the British Library

ISBN 13: 978-1-138-78725-4

Typeset in Baskerville
by Taylor & Francis Books

Publisher's Note
The publisher accepts responsibility for any inconsistencies that may have arisen during the conversion of this book from journal articles to book chapters, namely the possible inclusion of journal terminology.

Disclaimer
Every effort has been made to contact copyright holders for their permission to reprint material in this book. The publishers would be grateful to hear from any copyright holder who is not here acknowledged and will undertake to rectify any errors or omissions in future editions of this book.

Contents

Citation Information

The chapters in this book were originally published in *European Societies*, volume 15, issue 4 (October 2013). When citing this material, please use the original page numbering for each article, as follows:

Chapter 1
Editorial: Where are the PIGS? Still a Southern European
Welfare Regime?
Göran Therborn
European Societies, volume 15, issue 4 (October 2013) pp. 471–474

Chapter 2
The Southern European Welfare Model in the
Post-Industrial Order. Still a distinctive cluster?
Pau Marí-Klose and Francisco Javier Moreno-Fuentes
European Societies, volume 15, issue 4 (October 2013) pp. 475–492

Chapter 3
Youth, Family Change and Welfare Arrangements. Is the South still
so different?
Luis Moreno and Pau Marí-Klose
European Societies, volume 15, issue 4 (October 2013) pp. 493–513

Chapter 4
The Myth of Mediterranean Familism. Family values, family structure
and public preferences for state intervention in care
Inés Calzada and Clem Brooks
European Societies, volume 15, issue 4 (October 2013) pp. 514–534

Chapter 5
Bridge Over Troubled Waters. Family, gender and welfare in Portugal
in the European context
Anália Torres, Bernardo Coelho and Miguel Cabrita
European Societies, volume 15, issue 4 (October 2013) pp. 535–556

Chapter 6

Redefining the Dynamics of Intergenerational Family Solidarity in Spain
Jordi Caïs and Laia Folguera
European Societies, volume 15, issue 4 (October 2013) pp. 557–576

Chapter 7

The Southern European Migrant-Based Care Model. Long-term care and employment trajectories in Italy and Spain
Barbara Da Roit, Amparo González Ferrer and Francisco Javier Moreno-Fuentes
European Societies, volume 15, issue 4 (October 2013) pp. 577–596

Chapter 8

Is Social Protection in Greece at a Crossroads?
Maria Petmesidou
European Societies, volume 15, issue 4 (October 2013) pp. 597–616

Chapter 9

Female Employment and the Economic Crisis. Social change in Northern and Southern Italy
Alberta Andreotti, Enzo Mingione and Jonathan Pratschke
European Societies, volume 15, issue 4 (October 2013) pp. 617–635

Please direct any queries you may have about the citations to clsuk.permissions@cengage.com

Notes on Contributors

Alberta Andreotti is a Research Fellow in Economic Sociology at the University of Milan-Bicocca, Italy. She is also an Associate member of the program Cities are back in Town, based at Sciences-Po, Paris. Her research activities focus on social capital and social networks, urban poverty and local welfare systems, cities and middle classes, female employment with particular emphasis on the Italian North-South divide. She has published a book on social capital, chapters in edited volumes and several articles in international reviews (*AJEAS*, *IJURR*, *Urban Studies* and *Global Networks*).

Clem Brooks is Rudy Professor of Sociology at Indiana University, USA. His interests are in political sociology, comparative politics, political psychology, and quantitative methods. With Jeff Manza, he is the author of *Social Cleavages and Political Change*, *Why Welfare States Persist*, and *Whose Rights?*

Miguel Cabrita is Assistant Professor at ISCTE, Instituto Universitário de Lisboa and Reseacher at CIES-IUL. His main areas of teaching and research are contemporary sociological theories, the welfare-state and public policies, and more specifically family and social policy. He has participated in research projects on these topics, has also been involved in the evaluation of public and social policies in Portugal and is currently doing PhD research about fertility decisions.

Jordi Caïs is Senior Reader (Tenured) at the Department of Sociology at the University of Barcelona, Spain. He has a BA in Economics from the University of Barcelona, an MSc in European Social Policy from the London School of Economics and Political Science and a PhD in Sociology from the University of Barcelona. He did his PhD between the University of Barcelona and the University of California, San Diego thanks to a Fulbright Fellowship. His main areas of interest are comparative methodology and comparative social policy in the European region with a special focus on health, ageing and intergenerational relations. He has published in several journals and is author and co-author of seven books.

Inés Calzada is Researcher at the Spanish National Research Council and Lecturer of Sociology at Linköping University, Sweden. She works in topics related to comparative social policy, public opinion and migration.

Bernardo Coelho is a Sociologist and Researcher at CIES-IUL. He is also member of the CIEG (Interdisciplinary Centre for Gender Studies) executive committee. His current research interest are sociology of family, gender social relations, intimate life and sexuality, and sociology of financial markets. He is a Researcher of national and international research projects on these issues. Coelho is an author and co-author of articles and chapters in books. He published a book about prostitution (escort girls) in 2009. Currently he is preparing a PhD in Sociology at ISCTE-IUL (Instituto Universitário de Lisboa) on escort girls and their customers.

Barbara Da Roit is Assistant Professor in the Department of Sociology and Anthropology at the University of Amsterdam, the Netherlands. Her research focuses on changing care systems from a comparative perspective and looks at the mutual influence of social policies and care practices, with a specific interest on the changing nature of care work and the relationships between paid employment and the provision of informal care. Her book *Strategies of Care. Changing Elderly Care in Italy and the Netherlands* was published in 2010. She has published in international peer-reviewed journals (*SP&A, Current Sociology, Milbank Quarterly, Quality and Quantity, Social Politics, Ageing and Society, SESP, JESP*).

Laia Folguera is Assistant Lecturer in the Department of Sociology at the University of Barcelona (UB), Spain. She holds a PhD in Sociology from the UB and has specialized in qualitative research techniques, gender and masculinities. She has been a visiting student at the University of California, Berkeley; at the University of Essex; at the London School of Economics, and at Harvard University. She is the Convenor of the Working Groups of Sociology of Sexuality in the Congresses of the Spanish Federation of Sociology.

Amparo González Ferrer is Research Fellow at the Spanish National Research Council and member of the Research Group on Demographic Dynamics. She has extensively worked on international migration to Europe, with special attention to family-linked migration and labour market participation of immigrant women. She is currently coordinating a new project on the Life-course Expectations of Children of Immigrants in Spain (CHANCES), as well as participating in new research on return migration from the EU to origin areas.

Pau Marí-Klose is Assistant Professor at the University of Zaragoza, Spain and holds a BA in History (UB), a Masters in Social Sciences (Juan March Institute, Spain), an MA in Sociology (University of Chicago, USA), and a PhD in Sociology (UAM). His main interests lie in the study of inequalities and social policies such as child poverty, education, and intergenerational relations.

Enzo Mingione is Professor of Sociology at the University of Milano-Bicocca, Italy. He is President of Doctorate School SCISS (Studi Comparativi e Internazionali in Scienze Sociali). He has been the President of the RC on Urban and Regional Development, one of the Founders of the *International Journal of Urban and Regional Research*. His books include: *Fragmented Societies* (1991); (Ed) *Urban poverty and the Underclass* (1996); *Sociologia della Vita Economica* (1998); *Il Lavoro*, together with Enrico Pugliese (2010).

Luis Moreno is Research Professor at the Spanish National Research Council (IPP-CSIC) in Madrid. As a Political Sociologist, his two long-standing fields of research are: (a) social policy and welfare state; and (b) territorial politics (decentralisation, federalism, nationalism and Europeanisation). Both have been carried out from a comparative perspective. His books include: *The Territorial Politics of Welfare* (with N. McEwen, co-eds., 2005), *Diversity and Unity in Federal Systems* (with C. Colino, co-eds., 2010), and *La Europa asocial* (2012).

Francisco Javier Moreno-Fuentes is Research Fellow at CSIC and holds a BA in Sociology (UCM), a Masters in Social Sciences (Juan March Institute, Spain), an MSc in Social Policy (LSE, UK), and a PhD in Political Science (UAM, Spain). His research focuses on the comparative analysis of public policies in areas such as immigration, welfare regimes, and urban policies.

Maria Petmesidou is Professor of Social Policy at Democritus University of Thrace and Fellow of CROP/International Social Science Council. Her research interests are in the comparative analysis of social welfare, poverty and social exclusion in Southern Europe and the broader Mediterranean region; social stratification and social development; labour market and employment policies. She has published many books, chapters in edited volumes and articles in journals. Recent publications (in English): What future for the middle classes and 'inclusive solidarity' in *South Europe*, Global Social Policy, 2011; 'Southern Europe' in *International Handbook of the Welfare State*, Routledge, 2013; 'Is the crisis a watershed moment for the Greek welfare state? The chances for modernization amidst an ambivalent EU record on "Social Europe"', in *The Greek Crisis*, (forthcoming).

Jonathan Pratschke is Research Fellow in the Department of Economics and Statistics at the University of Salerno, Italy. His main research interests relate to the spatial articulation of social inequalities in relation to the labour market, housing, education, welfare and well-being. He has published books, chapters and journal articles in English and Italian, with a particular focus on the application of advanced statistical modelling techniques to social data.

Anália Torres, PhD in Sociology, is Full Professor of Sociology in ISCSP, School of Social and Political Sciences of the Technical University of Lisbon, Portugal, Head of the Sociology Unit, Researcher in CAPP (Centre for Administration & Public Policies) and Founder in ISCSP of the CIEG (Centre of Interdisciplinary Gender Studies). She was President of ESA (European

Sociological Association (2009–2011)). She has directed national and international research teams on family, gender, marriage, divorce, work and family, poverty, drug addition, youth and child protection system. She has published 16 books and more than 60 articles and chapters of books, some of them accessible in www.analiatorres.com.

INTRODUCTION
Where are the PIGS? Still a Southern European Welfare Regime?

This special issue, guest-edited by Francisco Javier Fuentes-Moreno and
Pau Marí-Klose, who have done an excellent job on it, brings into focus
social patterns and policies of the Southern Rim of Europe. Is there a
special Southern social pattern, comparable to the Nordic, Continental,
and Anglo-Saxon 'welfare regimes'? Or was it a transitory phenomenon, a
conceptual stopgap of the mid 1990s to cope with lacunae of the original
Trinitarian world of welfare capitalism?

This question has got a new political and socio-economic relevance with
the current debt and finance crisis of these countries, which economic
journalism has grouped together under the acronym of PIGS.

Accidental Coincidence?

Can the current crisis be interpreted as evidence of a common Southern or
Mediterranean social pattern? Caution and skepticism are called for here.
The causal paths to the crisis differ among the countries. To Greece a
main factor was public finance and public debt, to Spain it was a private
construction bubble that burst, and more meandering paths led to the
crises of Portugal and Italy. In neither case, did the welfare regime play
any significant role, as is shown by our authors, and indicated in the
overview below. The most straightforward commonality is that the PIGS,
as national societies and economies, are the four least developed, least
affluent members of the Eurozone (before its eastern enlargement),
benefiting from North-to-South capital inflows in the boom years but
hampered by the Zone rules in managing their loans when the
international crisis struck.

The contributions of the editors and the authors of this issue will
stimulate a renewed discussion of a Southern European social regime and
of the enduring fruitfulness of existing welfare typologies more generally.
As a first follow-up of the issue contributions, a few comparative
observations on the location of the South in European social relations of
today are offered here.

Familism

There is indeed a Southern commonality of family households, larger than the EU average, with more households of three or more adults and fewer living single, and fewer single parents. They share this pattern with Eastern EU, but the three-plus adults are clearly more frequent among the PIGS. Common is a structural familism (in a sense different from that used by Calzada and Brooks below) of household arrangements, rather than a traditional, religiously anchored value familism, which is rapidly eroding, as Torres et al. and Moreno and Marí-Klose point out. In the latter respect, only Greece stands out, with the lowest proportion by far of births outside marriage, whereas that share is well above EU average in Portugal, close to average in Spain, but substantially lower in Italy. Complexity and variation are highlighted by a finding of Moreno and Marí-Klose, that cohabitation before marriage is more frequent in Greece than in the rest of the South. All four have a fertility rate significantly lower than the EU rate, and Italy, Portugal, and Spain also have below average marriage rates.

The gendering of the labor markets is very different among the four countries. The gender gap of employment is much higher than the EU gap in Italy – due to its South, as Andreotti et al. emphasize in this issue –, whereas the Spanish and, very clearly, the Portuguese gap is smaller than average. Portugal in this respect is closer to Scandinavia than to Spain, not to speak of to Greece and Italy.

There is another Southern familism, seldom noticed, although touched upon by Da Roit et al. below, employer familism, private households employing domestic workers. The only part of Europe where this is a phenomenon of any significance at all, officially employing at least 4% of the female labor force, is the South, headed by Cyprus (9.7%) and Spain (8.4%), and including, in descending order, Portugal, Greece, France, and Italy.

The Welfare State

Whatever caused the public debt crisis in the South, it was not welfare profligacy. In fact, Greece, Spain, and Portugal spend much less on social protection per inhabitant than the EU27 (counted in purchasing power parities), Italy somewhat more, and all substantially less than other Euro countries. In comparison with the Eurozone in 2007, Italy spent 95% of the Zone average on social benefits, Greece 76%, Spain 74%, and Portugal 64%. Greek social spending was then 69% of the German out of a GDP economy per capita 78% of the German (See further Petmesidou below.) In other words, a certain commonality of relatively low spending in the Western European context, although in terms of GDP commitment, UK, Ireland, and Finland belong to the same group (taking the pre-crisis social expenditure GDP shares of 2007 as the best recent comparison). The difference to the neoliberal Eastern European states is substantial.

In terms of overall fiscal balance – of total government expenditure and revenue –, however, there was a common harbinger of problems. In the boom year of 2007, the Greek government ran a deficit of 6.8% of GDP, Portugal one of 3.1% of GDP, Italy had a deficit of 1.6% of GDP, and Spain 1.5%. The EU27 then had a fiscal balance of -0.9% of GDP and the Eurozone one of -0.7.

With regard to the structure of the welfare state, crude expenditure proportions, at least, do not indicate any particular Southern cluster. Three countries dedicate relatively more spending to old age protection than the average EU member, but so do also Austria, Sweden, and the UK. Italy is standing out alone (with Latvia) devoting more than half of all social benefits to old age pensioners. But Italy's Southern companion Spain gives one of the EU's smallest shares of social expenditure (a third) to the elderly. The Portuguese give almost as much as the Swedish to family and children (10 and 11%, respectively), while the other three countries spend less than the European average on them. While Italy devotes 1.5–3% of its social spending to unemployment compensation in 2007 and 2010, much below the Euro average (of 8% in 2010), Spain is the highest spender on it, 10% of all public social benefits in 2007, 14% in 2010.

Distributive Outcomes

The PIGS are all in the upper band of European income inequality, together with Bulgaria, Latvia, Lithuania, Romania, and the UK. But in, e.g., transatlantic terms, the intra-European national inequality differences are clearly smaller than those between; say the UK and the United States, Portugal and Brazil, or Spain and Argentina. The risk of relative poverty (below 60% of national median income) was already before the crisis somewhat higher in the South than in the core of Euroland, 8.5 percentage points in Greece, a few percentage points in the others, compared to the Franco-German core. By 2011, the same risk gap had widened to more 11 percentage points in Greece, almost 9 in Italy, to 8 in Spain, and to 5 points in Portugal.

What the Eurostat calls 'severe material deprivation' (defined both by absolute and relative measures) is in Europe an Eastern mass phenomenon, except in the Czech Republic and Slovenia. Before the crisis, Greece was the only Western country in which the fate befell on more than a tenth of the population. By 2011 it also hit 11% of Italians, whereas the Spanish figure for 2011 (3.9 severely materially deprived) was actually lower than those for France, Germany, and the UK (slightly above 5%).

Currently, in the summer of 2013, Greece, Spain, and Portugal have the three highest unemployment rates in Europe, and the Italian rate, though less than half of the Greek and the Spanish, is above Euro average. But this is a crisis effect. In 2006 Greece, Italy, Portugal, and Spain all had a lower unemployment rate than Germany and in 2007 only Portugal overtook Germany, by 0.2 percentage points. A structural labor market problem was discernible in the last boom year, though. Greece, Portugal, and Italy had the highest youth unemployment rate in Western Europe, and Spain was not far behind, although with a lower rate than France and Sweden.

Envoi

It seems that there are some significant enduring features of Southern European structures, of households, states, economies, and labor markets, deriving from similarities of modern history. But attitudes, values, and policies look much more susceptible to change, sometimes very rapidly. Sociologists had better be cautious in relying on attitudes and values.

However, in the world of scholarship, no big question is answered by an editorial. The debate will continue on the many questions raised by the contributors in this issue. Many thanks to Francisco Javier Fuentes-Moreno, to Pau Marí-Klose, and to their authors.

References

There is no space here for tables and lists of references. The comparisons above are all based on Eurostat online data, except for employed domestic labor, which is from ILO, *Domestic workers across the world* (2013, www.ilo.org), and the note on transatlantic income inequality differences, which also refer to the US Congressional Budget Office and the Luxemburg Income Study.

Göran Therborn

THE SOUTHERN EUROPEAN WELFARE MODEL IN THE POST-INDUSTRIAL ORDER

Still a distinctive cluster?

Pau Marí-Klose
Departamento de Psicología y Sociología, Universidad de Zaragoza
Francisco Javier Moreno-Fuentes
Institute of Public Goods and Policies (IPP-CSIC), Madrid, Spain

ABSTRACT: The discussion on the existence of a distinctive 'Mediterranean' welfare model has focused on the historical and politico-institutional dynamics, as well as on the policy traits of the welfare arrangements found in Southern European countries. Particular attention has been given to the external pressures and internal constraints faced by the welfare systems of these countries, as well as to what extent there is a common response to such challenges. In this article, we claim that while researchers were embarked in this scholarly effort, Southern European societies kept changing, transforming the nature of existing arrangements in not always forecasted directions, to the point of questioning the adequacy of clustering them under a common type. The current context of economic and financial crisis introduces additional factors in the process of transformation and reform of the welfare schemes of these countries, placed at the epicentre of the turmoil shattering European economies and societies.

1. The architecture of the South European welfare (as we know it)[1]

In a seminal article written in the mid 1990s, Ferrera drew attention to the poor characterisation of the Mediterranean welfare state in the scholarly literature (Ferrera 1996). Latin countries (and especially Spain, Portugal

---

1. This article was drafted within the SOLFCARE project ('*Solidaridad familiar, cambio actitudinal y reforma del Estado de bienestar en España: el familismo en transición*'), under the 'Plan Nacional de I + D + i, Spain' (CSO2011-27494).

and Greece) remained out of the scope of observation in many of the main works on welfare states published in the 1980s and early 1990s (Flora 1986; Esping-Andersen 1990). The few scholars interested in the Latin rim usually focused on the 'rudimentary' character of welfare programs, the strong influence of Catholicism and its social doctrine, as well as in the central role attributed to the family in the provision of welfare.

Thanks to Ferrera, and a significant number of mostly Southern European researchers, our understanding of the organisational features and overall functioning logic of the Mediterranean model improved significantly. They sketched out the unique historical and policy traits that place this regime apart from others, particularly the Continental welfare regime with which it undoubtedly shares many commonalities. They also recognised the politico-institutional dynamics derived from the distinctive welfare arrangements found in the Mediterranean countries. Growing attention has been given to external pressures and internal constraints faced by Mediterranean welfare states, as well as to what extent there is a distinctive 'Mediterranean' response to such challenges. While researchers were embarked in this scholarly effort, societies in Italy, Spain, Greece and Portugal kept changing, transforming the nature of existing arrangements in not always forecasted directions. Do the countries of the Latin rim still belong to the same and distinctive cluster?

It is not easy to give a clear-cut answer to this question. There is little doubt that, in the early 1990s, at the precise moment that the literature on the welfare state was endorsing the threefold partition of the worlds of welfare into the 'Anglo-Saxon', 'Scandinavian' and 'Continental' varieties, the four Southern Europe nations were reaching their peak of commonality, supporting the claim that there was a fourth regime that had been unduly ignored by mainstream research. Such commonality was founded not only in a shared cultural heritage, but also in a distinctive pathway to modernity. Mediterranean societies had had to wait until the 1960s to undergo a process of rapid and highly compressed modernisation, involving not only their economies, but also the social, cultural and political dimensions. In this atypical process, the resulting interplay between the main 'pillars' of welfare provision (labour market, welfare state and family) acquired rather distinctive characteristics, creating a number of distortions and unresolved problems that apparently have also produced a series of relatively common social strains and tensions.

1.1. The Mediterranean labour market

It is undeniable that the Mediterranean labour market, as portrayed in the seminal works on the Mediterranean welfare model, exhibits certain common traits with the Continental type, beginning with the relatively high unemployment rates (the welfare-without-work syndrome), and the relatively low female participation in the labour force. This not withstanding, some institutional profiles were rather unique to these countries, notably the existence of a clear insider/outsider cleavage. During their industrialisation processes Southern European countries put in place highly protective employment regimes, especially against dismissal of workers from core sectors of the economy (i.e. public administration, large industries, etc.). Stringent employment protection legislation has often been conceptualised as a legacy of the authoritarian/corporatist ideologies influencing policy-makers in the pre-war (Italy) and after-war periods (in the three other countries), and as a consequence of the slow development of unemployment compensation systems (fully introduced only in the 1980s). It has also been argued that the democratic governments that took power in the 1970s and early 1980s in Portugal, Greece and Spain refrained from dismantling the labour legislation inherited from the authoritarian past out of fear for the potential social unrest that could destabilise the transition towards a new political regime (Karamessini 2008).

Thanks to the rigid employment protection legislation enjoyed by workers at the core (most of them males prime-age and older), these groups had high job stability and 'family wages' with strong links to seniority. At the other end of the spectrum, in more peripheral sectors (including a large number of underground economy firms) continuous flows in and out of employment are the norm. Fixed-term contracts, seasonal employment, free-lance activities and internships have provided uneven professional opportunities to a large segment of the workforce (young workers, women and immigrants) under conditions of weak attachment to the labour market, low remuneration, and often lousy working conditions.

As unemployment soared in the late 1970s and early 1980s, governments launched labour deregulation reforms, but each of them chose its own path towards labour market flexibility. Portuguese and Spanish governments introduced measures facilitating the unrestricted use of fixed-term contracts, resulting in a sharp rise in temporary employment and the reinforcement of labour market segmentation. Greek and Italian governments also relaxed the use of fixed-term contracts, but the scope of the reforms they implemented was more limited and the consequences smaller (OECD 2004).In fact during the 1980s temporary employment fell in Greece and it remained low in Italy.

The dual structure of the labour market in Spain, and to a lesser extent in Portugal, encouraged firms to adopt flexibilisation strategies based in the principle of 'last hired, first fired'. In times of economic slowdown, temporary workers assumed the consequences of firms' labour readjustment (Saint Paul 1996). For example, the economic crisis of the first half of the 1990s, as well as the current economic troubles affecting the Spanish economy, brought youth unemployment rates well over 40% as a result of the destruction of temporary jobs held by the more recent entrants in the labour market. In Italy and Greece the concentration of unemployment risk in the group of temporary workers has been less paramount, although dualism is also a hallmark of their labour markets.

1.2. The Mediterranean welfare state

If we look at the general traits of Southern European welfare states (their scope, financing logics, and underlying organisational features), we could say that this model has many elements in common with the Continental model, while it also shares a few characteristics with the Northern European universalistic type. Cash benefits (especially pensions) have traditionally played a prominent role in the provision of public welfare in Southern Europe. As in 'Bismarkian' regimes, income maintenance is essentially work-related, based both on occupational status and on previous contributions. In line with corporatist countries, the system of social assistance is also weak, offering low levels of protection to citizens not covered by employment-related schemes. In contrast, education and healthcare constitute universal entitlements, basically guaranteed to all citizens (residents) along the lines of the Scandinavian systems.

One of the distinguishing features of this model is supposed to be its fragmentation. As Ferrera (1996) points out, a large number of separate income-maintenance schemes exist in Greece and Italy, some of them very broad and general (i.e. covering 'industrial workers' as a single category), others circumscribed to narrow professional groups. This author recognises that this portrait can hardly be extended to Spain and Portugal, where the level of fragmentation is similar to Continental standards. The main exception are disparate and poorly coordinated non-contributory programmes and services catering for groups defined as deserving beneficiaries (orphans, widows, disabled), leaving other vulnerable groups (new entrants in labour markets, workers in the underground economy, long-term unemployed, inactive people providing informal care to dependants, undocumented migrants, etc.) ineligible for social assistance.

The most distinctive trait emerging of the combinations of dual labour markets and highly fragmented social protection systems is a clear polarisation between well-protected beneficiaries, and a large group of under-/unprotected workers and citizens (Ferrera 1996; Moreno 2006). Some categories of employees (white collar workers, core blue collar workers in medium and large enterprises with permanent contracts, public employees) received relatively generous benefits for short-term social risks (sickness, maternity, temporary unemployment spells), and relatively generous earning-related pensions, while a large segment of citizens remain vulnerable in relation to those same risks. The strong age-bias orientation of social policies epitomises this situation. While older workers (and the elderly in general) are relatively well protected, younger workers and families remain largely out of the safety net. Youth favouring policies (housing benefits or affordable social housing, childcare, economic support for young households with children) or active labour policies for new entrants into the job market have remained underdeveloped. Italy, Spain and Greece, have the most heavily elderly oriented welfare states in the OECD, with Portugal not far from them (Lynch 2006).

1.3. The Mediterranean family

It has often been argued that welfare and family are much more closely intertwined in Mediterranean countries than in any other welfare regimes. According to this view, the historical presence of strong family ties, and the existence of a familistic value system, constituted the cornerstone of welfare provision, and has had a decisive influence in social-policy making in these countries. The strong institutionalisation of marriage, the availability of full-time housewives, and the intensity of family ties across generations enabled the State to delegate the responsibility for guaranteeing basic economic security and to provide for the care-giving needs of large segments of unprotected citizens, thus helping to keep the political demands for better public provision low. Families functioned traditionally as 'shock absorbers' when its members confronted short-term deprivation (unemployment, family breakdown), or special needs (sickness, dependency or maternity). The State was not expected to intervene, but to concentrate on the protection of the heads of the family. Resource-pooling and inter-generational solidarity expectations within the family also deactivated demands for the de-segmentation of labour markets.

The familistic ethos has been backed by the social doctrine of the Catholic Church, which not only had an important cultural influence, but also played a prominent role in the field of social policy in Italy, Spain and Portugal (wile the Greek Orthodox Church played a functionally equivalent role). The strong emphasis in the role of the family has not been accompanied by social policies that supported families, or strengthened their capacity to care for its members. Rather, the reference to the responsibilities of the family served to legitimise the provision of meagre social services, as well as to overtly justify political inaction in these areas of policies (Saraceno 1994). These characteristics set the Mediterranean model apart from Continental European countries where, although there is a strong reliance on the family for the provision of care to its members (based on the principle of subsidiarity), the family receives financial support to better perform these roles (Bettio and Plattenga 2004).

2. Southern Europe at the turn of the millennium

While scholars were still highlighting the commonalities in the institutional profiles of the Southern European countries, the newly labelled *regime* was already showing growing signs of internal differentiation. In the context of the economic and political changes of the 1990s, the four countries entered (each at its own pace) into a new stage in which their traditional welfare equilibriums became growingly de-stabilised. At the change were the common external pressures (notably globalisation and European integration), as well as the internal challenges posed by the transformation of their domestic economic and social environments. The paths of institutional adaptation to these challenges varied considerably, placing the four countries in diverse reform trajectories.

Globalisation and Europeanisation exposed countries to common opportunities and constraints. The integration of financial markets restricted national governments' margin of manoeuvre to levy the necessary funds to establish new social programmes by weakening the State's control over national tax bases, and by increasing the costs of financing fiscal deficits. In a context of increased 'exit options', it became more difficult for governments to promote economic environments that guarantee high returns to investors without jeopardising regulatory frameworks and social policies that enjoy wide social support. Faced with these constraints, small differences in the chosen policy options may produce large differences in policy trajectories.

During the 2000s, Southern Europe countries followed different economic developmental paths. While growth continued in Spain and Greece (boosted in both cases by a sharp fall in nominal interests rates in the Euro-zone, and the flow of European structural aid in the case of Greece), it stalled in Italy and Portugal. The effects of global pressures were particularly severe in Portugal, which experienced a dramatic recession with a profound impact on its public finances. The emergence of new players in world trade, as well as the enlargement of the EU towards the East, resulted especially damaging to the Portuguese economy because of its specialisation on relatively unsophisticated labour intensive manufacturing (Royo 2013).

Alongside these global factors, European integration also prompted fiscal austerity and the recalibration of welfare policies. The path towards Monetary Union, with its 'convergence criteria', forced a shift towards more rigorous fiscal policies in order to 'join Europe'. Not all Southern European countries showed the same commitment to austerity though. Steps aiming at cost containment and towards the reorganisation of welfare provision were taken in Italy, Spain and Portugal, implying the restructuration of benefits to counter unfavourable demographics, and the attenuation of privileges for hyper-protected groups (i.e. pensioners in Italy). The Spanish government was one of the most disciplined pupils, allowing a certain margin to expand in previously undeveloped welfare areas (support for families and fight against social exclusion). At the opposite end public deficits increased in Greece even with robust economic growth (public deficits decreased from 9.2% in 1995, to 3.2% in 1999, 'meeting' the convergence criteria, skyrocketing after the fiscal belt was softened – between 2000 and 2005, public deficits run above 5% annually, and public debt went beyond 130% of the GDP). Among the causes for the lack of fiscal discipline observed in this country was the failure to reform the clientelistic structures of its welfare system (Petmesidou and Mossialos 2005; Matsaganis 2011).

The second source of pressures for Southern European welfare regimes was linked to the transformation of domestic labour markets and social contexts. During the 1990s and early 2000s, these countries experienced an (uncompleted) transition towards a new 'post-industrial' order, which altered occupational structures, as well as family and gender relations. Among other changes, two developments deserve particular attention. First, employment in agriculture and manufacturing accelerated its decline, and services became the main driver of occupational expansion. In this decade the proportion of citizens working in the service sector reached more than half of the working population and kept growing rapidly. The emerging service economy opened new employment opportunities for women and other 'outsiders' (especially new migrants from developing countries), but often at a heavy cost in terms of the quality of those newly created jobs. Low wages and poor-quality jobs had a particularly hard impact on the lives of young people in Southern Europe, and a large number of young people faced major difficulties to reach financial independence, and therefore to exit the parental household. As a result, the Mediterranean youth delayed couple formation, and become first-time parents later than in the rest of Western Europe, thus driving fertility rates to unprecedented low levels. Young families are formed later in the life cycle, and their average size has become considerably smaller.[2]

In addition to changes in employment structures, the transformation in demographics and social environments had considerable implications in

2. This is partly due to a fall in fertility, but also to the growing residential autonomy of the elderly.

these countries. The rise in female employment in post-industrial labour market increased the number of dual earner households, where the family status of the male breadwinner is challenged by the existence of a second source of income (a key asset to maintain desired consumption standards), increasing the difficulties that these families have in reconciling work and family life. Financial autonomy gives women new bargaining capacities, which are prompting rapid changes in gender relations within families, and straining couple relationships, increasingly judged unsatisfactory. In these conditions welfare equilibriums operating under the presumption that care and domestic work would be performed by full-time housewives on an unpaid basis cannot longer be sustained. These equilibriums become less viable because of the growing 'precarisation' of marriage linked to the inclination of many young couples to rely on less stable forms of partnership, as well as the rapidly climbing divorce rates among younger cohorts.

The growing precariousness of employment and social relationships in countries that were not accustomed to fluidity in these domains are bringing to the fore new problems and dilemmas. It is increasingly evident that Southern European countries are not vaccinated against the *new social risks* (NSR) widely described in other European countries (Taylor Gooby 2004; Armingeon and Bonoli 2006). A growing number of people in Southern Europe struggle daily against the consequences of intermittent labour careers, being stuck in a low-skill low-wage occupation (or in a job for which the worker is overqualified), having skills and training that become obsolete, being badly protected against disability or unemployment as a result of an unstable job career, becoming frail and lacking family support, being unable to balance paid work and family responsibilities, becoming a lone parent, etc. NSR, which were virtually absent in Southern Europe before the 1990s, both as a condition bear by a significant amount of people, and as a matter of public discussion, have gained prominence, feeding new discourses on social policy as well as new political dynamics.

The newly acquired prominence of NSR in the political agenda derives only partly from the demographic weight of those who more directly bear these risks (Bonoli 2005). As shown later in Moreno and Mari-Klose's article, NSR and demands related to socio-economic transformations have had a fairly unequal salience in Southern European countries. Their role in framing new political debates about welfare provision in an era of increasing global pressures and budgetary austerity explains their growing relevance. Policies targeting NSR often aim at changing welfare 'as we know it' by promoting spending commitments that 'pay off', and eventually helping re-scale traditional welfare state programmes for 'old risks'. This makes some of these policies appealing to broad constituencies, which include NSR bearers (often left leaning voters), but also other social and political actors interested in the elimination of perceived 'sources of inefficiency' within the welfare system (i.e., employers, policy experts). The economic benefits of these policies are such that they may favour the formation of broad advocacy coalitions, thus generating new opportunities for policy making. As Bonoli (2005) points out, the outputs of the politics of NSR coverage often take the shape of the inclusion of initiatives of cost containment or retrenchment (in policy areas providing coverage for 'old risks'), and of ('affordable') improvement in the provision of schemes that address NSR, within a single reform.

Three additional factors contributed to open windows of opportunity for reform in areas related to the coverage of NSR in Southern Europe. The first were a series of intellectual inputs coming from EU institutions. During the 1990s, new scholarly understandings of the challenges faced by the 'European social model', as well as ideas and policy solutions to modernise public provision, informed EU directives and recommendations. From there, they poured down into the national political debates, shaping the reflection on the shortcomings of the national welfare states, and re-orienting political attention towards NSR. Certain reforms of social insurance schemes implemented in Italy and Spain (extending compulsory insurance to workers hired under non-standard contracts, or removing penalisations for workers with interrupted and fragmented careers) reflected these concerns for NSR (Jessoula 2007). European guidelines also had a strong influence on policy shifts that involved gender and family issues following EU Directives regulating maternity protection (1992), and parental leave (1996) (Treib and Falkner 2004). The strong commitment shown by some Mediterranean countries to follow these guidelines can be interpreted as the expression of the wish of 'late comer' members to 'catch up' to median EU figures and indicators.

The second factor playing a noticeable role in the salience of NSR was the return to power of left-of centre parties after spending a long time in opposition (Bonoli 2005). In line with what had occurred in other European countries, the pressures to adopt policies that would be noticeably different from those of their predecessors pushed the new left-of-centre governments to advance policies providing coverage for NSR, albeit again with different degrees of commitment. The Zapatero governments in Spain appear as the most ambitious in this respect, answering to high expectations for social policy expansion from its voters after nearly a decade of economic growth and fiscal restraint under the previous Conservative governments. From the mid 2000s onwards, Zapatero's government introduced a wide range of measures to favour NSR bearers, including initiatives to favour the residential autonomy of young people, to promote female employment and the conciliation of work and family life (through an expansion of childcare and elderly care), and to encourage fertility and help young families through birth grants (Ferrera 2010; Moreno and Marí-Klose 2013).[3] Social protection expenditure on family/children increased well above the European average between 2004 and 2010 (36% over the six-year period, only below the Irish growth in EU-15) (Eurostat 2013). In a climate of economic optimism such measures represented a significant departure from traditional welfare arrangements in Southern Europe. However, expansion along these lines did not last long enough to ensure institutional resilience. Reforms came to a sudden halt in 2008 with the eruption of the financial and economic crisis. In the face of mounting budgetary pressures, the Spanish government opted to put their efforts at saving the core of welfare provision, subjecting the newly created policies targeting NSR to major cutbacks.[4]

The third factor is the activity of regional governments in providing innovative responses to NSR. Decentralisation of substantial welfare responsibilities, coupled with new arrangement for fiscal autonomy, provided the impetus for the expansion of new welfare policies. Regional initiatives pushed welfare growth through 'demonstration effects' and learning processes. Thus, areas of social services in Spain and Italy significantly expanded following decentralisation, resulting in increasing inter-regional divergence in social rights and entitlements later minimised through emulation practices (Moreno 2011). These processes raised concerns about fiscal sustainability, as each regional administration aimed at showing its capability of providing top-class services to be 'no less' than other regions.

3. Economic crisis and the future of the Mediterranean Welfare regime

One of the main characteristics of the current financial and economic crisis is its capacity to reveal the weaknesses of the economic, social and political institutional environments of each country. In the USA, the crisis exposed the irrational nature of speculative banking practices (producing large financial and real state bubbles), and the flaws of the productive

---

3. Along the same lines, the Socialist government of Socrates in Portugal introduced policies supporting the conciliation of family and work through generous parental leaves and a 'daddy month' that emulated the Scandinavian arrangements (Tavora 2012).

4. Zapatero first, and Rajoy's Conservative government later, concentrated many of their budget cuts on policies targeting NSR. In 2010, Zapatero eliminated the birth grant (2500€ for families of newborns and newly adopted children), and curtailed assistance to young people moving out of parental home. Rajoy's government drained resources devoted to the Law of Dependency and to childcare policies, seriously compromising their sustainability.

sector (decreasing competitiveness, international trade deficits, accumulation of public and private debt) (Stiglitz 2010). In the EU it pointed at the huge imbalances within the countries of the Euro zone, and at the flaws in the design of this common currency area (no coordination mechanisms for economic and fiscal policies) (Pisani–Ferry 2012).

Challenging the positive vision of globalisation that prevailed in the previous decade, and within an increasingly neo–Malthusian atmosphere (scarcity of natural resources, threat of energy and environmental shocks), the crisis introduced in the public and political agendas the debate on the future of Western societies in front to the emergence of the 'BRICS'. The delocalisation of large number of jobs to countries with lower salaries (initially low-skilled, but gradually more qualified), weaker environmental regulations, and little social protection seriously questioned the economic systems of Western European countries. This was particularly true for Southern Europe, countries that greatly benefited of their participation in the Euro during the first years of the functioning of the common currency[5] at the expense of accumulating significant unbalances that weakened the foundations of their economies.[6] With their productivity decreasing, their competitive position in global markets significantly deteriorated, and their fiscal balance increasingly compromised, the financial shock adopted the form of a sovereign–debt crisis in these countries (international investors speculating about the capacity of the 'PIGS' to service their debt,[7] and betting on the break-up of the Euro-zone).

As public and private actors changed their investment and consumption strategies economies slowed down, real state bubbles busted, unemployment soared, and fiscal revenues collapsed in the periphery of the Euro-zone. State's initiatives to bail out banks (responsible of facilitating the accumulation of private debt and fuelling real state bubbles), and public policies aimed at reducing the effects of the 'credit-crunch' on the 'real economy', together with public efforts to minimise the most extreme

---

5. A stable financial environment (easier access to foreign creditors, historically low interest rates) facilitated the growth of their economies and their convergence with the more advanced European countries (increases in GDP per capita, activity rates, female participation in the labour market).

6. The 'illusion of wealth' resulted in uncompetitive costs structures due to structural inflation differentials, growing trade deficits, a substantial increase of debt (in different combinations of public and private), the development of real state bubbles, an acceleration of investment in infrastructures (sometimes without the adequate cost-benefit analysis), and the arrival of significant immigration flows to occupy the niches of the labour market not wanted by autochthonous workers.

7. The assumption that 'the flying PIGS eventually had to land' has predominated in the media and public opinions of Northern European countries, impregnating the political narrative on the crisis and its solution.

effects of the crisis (unemployment benefits) aggravated the situation of public finances. Political discourses calling for the reduction of public spending, and the implementation of strict austerity measures in Southern Europe, openly recommended the reduction of social rights and welfare entitlements. The EU and IMF programs to bail out the governments of Greece, Ireland, and Portugal included precise demands for cutbacks in social protection programs (pensions, health care and subsidies). The austerity plans signed at the EU level with the objective of sending a clear message to the 'markets', and to reduce the pressure over sovereign debts also came with clear 'recommendations' to introduce structural reforms (in labour markets regulations, pension schemes and other basic welfare programs) that were supposed to facilitate the development of more 'virtuous' economic models in these countries.

The current crisis is clearly operating as an 'analyser', revealing the weak points of the institutional equilibriums of the Mediterranean Welfare regime. The accession to power of Conservative governments in the four Southern European countries took place in a social climate favouring the adoption of 'emergency measures' (especially in the Iberian countries), thus opening a 'window of opportunity' for the redefinition of social protection schemes. The deterioration in the quality of service provision due to cost-containment measures (widely felt across these four countries), the introduction of (additional) co-payments, combined with encourage-ment to subscribe private insurance may weaken the support for public welfare provision (especially among middle classes that can afford private solutions), eventually opening the gate for deeper welfare retrenchment. The role of families as 'shock absorbers', cushioning extreme forms of social exclusion, constitutes a crucial aspect in this respect. Family micro-solidarity is unlikely to provide support to the extent it did in previous crisis (when family ties and familistic expectations were stronger, and male bread-winners were protected by stringent labour market regulations). The losers from this radical economic overhaul may struggle against the consequences of this crisis in a different world in which resource pooling within families may be less effective in lifting people out of poverty than they had been in the past.

While the countries included under this typology followed relatively divergent trends in recent times, to some extent putting into question the adequacy of the categorisation of a Mediterranean regime, the current situation may strengthen the 'path-dependency' patterns of those social protection systems, re-enforcing the commonalities shared by their welfare systems while diluting some of the most innovative developments implemented in this region in the years immediately before the crisis.

4. Structure of the Special issue

The articles presented in this Special Issue examine the recent evolution of the Mediterranean Welfare regime, and how the current financial challenges may contribute to redefine its basic traits in the near future. From the macro comparative analysis of long-term socio-demographic trends, to the study of specific welfare programs in a country, these papers use a variety of methods and approaches to review the specificities of the Mediterranean Welfare regime. They also share an interest in analysing the role that the transformations experienced by Southern European societies in recent years may have had over the defining boundaries of this Welfare regime ideal-type. In this respect, the analysis of some of the most important social and demographic transformations experienced by these societies, such as the ageing of the population, the increasing participation of women in the labour market, the decreasing expectations about care within the family at old age, and/or the role of migration to respond to some of the challenges posed by these transformations, constitute a structuring argument for the contributions included in this volume.

A second argument that cuts across several of the articles of this Special Issue is the relation between social values and the main characteristics of the Mediterranean Welfare regime, and how the relation between societal and value change, and the evolution of welfare policies in these countries can be analyzed. Some of the basic characteristics of this regime type are supposed be strongly grounded in axiological foundations of these societies (familistic tendencies, clientelism, lack of generalised trust, etc.). The extent to which those values may actually diverge from those of the rest of Europe, and whether they may have evolved in recent years as a consequence of the modernisation process experienced by these societies (Calzada *et al.* 2013), may also be extremely relevant when analysing the evolution of welfare schemes in Southern European countries.

The impact of the current fiscal and economic crisis on the Welfare regimes of these countries constitutes a third analytical axis for the papers included in this volume. This last aspect emerges as particularly important, since it is linked to the issue of the allegiance of citizens to the social contract in which the State guarantees basic social rights financed through (more or less) progressive taxation systems in exchange for legitimacy of the political system. This is especially relevant in a region that experienced a process of transition towards democratic regimes only (relatively) recently and where the risk of de-legitimatisation of the political systems/regimes/parties seems to be particularly important.

The first of the papers included in this Special Issue examines the extent to which some of the features that cluster South European countries into a distinctive Welfare regime may actually be blurring, prompted by changes in the interface between new attitudes, expectations and practices, and the public and private provision of social policies. As Moreno and Mari-Klose point out, the interaction between families, the State, and the market in the Mediterranean Welfare regime has been traditionally based on the existence of a strong household micro-solidarity. Supported in the caring work of women, this arrangement has provided high levels of self-perceived well-being at the expense of erratic careers or women's full withdrawal from the labour market. After a comparative analysis of socio-demographic trends in Europe, these authors point out how new lifestyles and social needs of younger generations are challenging the capacity of the family to continue functioning as 'shock absorber' and supplier of informal care. In this new scenario Southern European countries are caught in the choice of maintaining deep-seated cultural arrangements, or promoting new welfare programs to accommodate the demands and aspirations of younger cohorts. The pace and scope of these social transformations differs quite considerable across countries though, increasing the degree of internal variation within the Mediterranean regime and, quite significantly, the intra-variation within each country.

The contribution of Calzada and Brooks analyses the extent to which patterns of family structure and values in Europe appear to be connected to ideal-typical regimes, as predicted by the Welfare regimes and the gender/family relations literatures. These authors focus their analysis of European attitudes towards welfare policies on the study of the relation between the pattern of family structure/values and the attitudes towards service-oriented welfare states. Their analysis tests the hypothesis that family values and attitudes depress support for public interventions in this area of policy. By paying particular attention to the Mediterranean regime they show how, contrary to what could be derived from the literature on the topic, the relationship between family values and attitudes toward government child care provision is clearly positive. Far from eroding support for public child care services, family values appear to increase preferences for public provision in this area of policy.

Torres, Coelho and Cabrita's article also focuses on the change in family patterns, values and practices in Southern European countries and the political responses to those changes, particularly in Portugal. The authors claim that social scientists should update old categories of analysis to understand the changes that are transforming these societies in fundamental ways. In their view the indiscriminate use of old familistic frameworks is contributing to portray a distorted image of these societies. The article identifies drivers of change in Portugal, both at the demographic level (a new generation of better educated and cosmopolitan generations) and the political level (centre-left governments). Current trends prompt a convergence with Europe. But the authors are cautious in pointing out that such convergence is incomplete. Institutional constraints, especially regarding public welfare provision, continue to place a heavy burden on women's backs along 'traditional' lines.

The paper by Caïs and Folguera analyses the changes in intergenerational dynamics of family solidarity in Spain, and the factors (reciprocity, affection or duty) that affect the willingness to provide care for elderly dependent relatives. Through the combination of quantitative and qualitative empirical evidence they study the way in which changes in family dynamics, higher female labor market participation, the scarcity of public services, and the high cost of private services are affecting family caregiving strategies in this country. They conclude that the Mediterranean Welfare regime appears as increasingly ineffective. The sustainability of the Spanish elderly care model seems particularly troubled by the current context of budget austerity and retrenchment of the incipient policies developed in recent years.

The fifth paper by Da Roit, González and Moreno-Fuentes, analyses the relation between long-term-care policies and female employment in the care sector. Policies in this domain appear weak and fragmented in Southern Europe when compared to other regimes. The authors claim that it is precisely this weakness that can be considered responsible for the emergence of an informal care market staffed by migrant workers, often undocumented, and trapped in the underground economy. This situation, studied for the cases of Italy and Spain, has important implications for the development of long-term-care policies in these countries by defining an unregulated, precarious (and cheaper) scheme for the provision of care at the expense of the working conditions of the care-providers, their professionalisation, and the quality of care provided.

The paper by Petmesidou, centred on the study of the case of Greece, examines the limitations and deadlocks of welfare patterns embedded in the statist-familistic Welfare regime that for a long-time was pivotal for the institutional set up and social redistribution in that country. The cumulative nature of the social protection schemes built over several decades, and the effects of the current sovereign debt crisis on the Greek Welfare system, are analysed in an article reviewing the main reforms recently introduced under the pressure of foreign creditors.

The last paper of the volume by Andreotti, Mignone and Pratschke focuses on the Italian internal variation in female labour market participation and family responsibilities equilibriums. The goal of the paper is to challenge the image of a linear, continuous and convergent change in gender relations in Italy. The two distinct social 'sub-models' identified by the authors (related to distinct forms of modernisation) have far reaching consequences for gender relations and the well-being of households. Women in Northern Italy face increasing problems to reconcile professional and family responsibilities, and the delicate inter-generational solidarity arrangements look increasingly precarious. In the South, in contrast, large reserves of mostly low-qualified women remain outside the labour market in a state of discouragement, placing their households at risk of falling below the poverty line. The economic crisis has brought tensions within each model, accentuating differences between the regions, thus intensifying the need for policy innovation while obstructing the development of coherent policy responses.

During the 1990s and early 2000, a group of scholars established research on the Southern Europe Welfare model as a fertile ground for comparative analysis. Their views on the distortions introduced by the shared cultural traits of the Mediterranean countries, as well as by their distinctive pathways to modernity are worth revisiting today. The tensions and strains currently experienced by these countries exhibit a multifaceted nature and are to a great extent the consequence of recent developments, only partially linked to that common heritage. In this context it is of utmost importance that social sciences review and update frequently unquestioned understandings to contribute informing public debates and policy decision making in a balanced and productive manner.

References

Armingeon, K. and Bonoli, G. (eds) (2006) *The Politics of Post-Industrial Welfare States*, London: Routledge.

Bettio, F. and Plattenga, J. (2004) 'Comparing care regimes in Europe', *Feminist Economics* 10(2): 137–71.

Bonoli, G. (2005) 'The politics of new social policies: Providing coverage against new social risks in mature welfare states', *Policy and Politics* 33(3): 431–49.

Calzada, I., Gómez, M., Moreno, L. and Moreno-Fuentes, F. J. (2013) 'Regímenes de bienestar y valores en Europa', *Revista Española de Investigaciones Sociológicas* 141: 61–90.

Esping-Andersen, G. (1990) *The Three Worlds of Welfare Capitalism*, Cambridge: Polity Press.

Eurostat (2013) http://epp.eurostat.ec.europa.eu/portal/page/portal/eurostat/home

Ferrera, M. (2010) 'The South European countries', in F. G. Castles, S. Leibfried and J. Lewis (eds), *The Oxford Handbook of the Welfare State*, New York: Oxford University Press, pp. 616–29.

Ferrera, M. (1996) 'The "Southern Model" of welfare in social Europe', *Journal of European Social Policy* 6(1): 17–37.

Flora, P. (1986) *Growth to Limits: The European Welfare States Since World War II*. Vols. *3*, Berlin: De Gruyter.

Jessoula, M. (2007) 'Italy: An uncompleted departure from Bismark', Working paper 4/07, Dipartamento di Studi Sociali e Politici, Università degli Studi di Milano.

Karamessini, M. (2008) 'Continuity and change in the Southern European social model', *International Labour Review* 147(1): 44–69.

Lynch, J. (2006) *Age in the Welfare State: The Origins of Social Spending on Pensioners, Workers, and Children*, New York: Cambridge University Press.

Matsaganis, M. (2011) 'The welfare state and the crisis: The case of Greece', http://www.ecprnet.eu/MyECPR/proposals/reykjavik/uploads/papers/2180.pdf.

Moreno, L. (2011) 'Multilevel citizens, new social risks and regional welfare', Institute of Public Goods and Polices Working Paper Series Number 3, CCHS-CSIC.

Moreno, L. (2006) 'The model of social protection in southern Europe: Enduring characteristics?', in Social welfare reforms in Europe: Challenges and strategies in continental and Southern Europe, special issue for the 60th anniversary of Revue Française des Affaires Sociales, No 1 (Ja.–Feb), pp. 73–95.

Moreno, L. and Marí-Klose, P. (2013) 'Las Transformaciones del Estado de bienestar Mediterráneo: Trayectorias y retos de un régimen en Transicion', in E. del Pino and M. Josefa rubio (eds), *Los Estados de bienestar en la Encrucijada*, Madrid: Technos, pp. 126–46.

OECD (2004) *Employment Outlook*, Paris: OECD.

Petmesidou, M. and Mossialos, E. (2005) *Social Policy Development in Greece*, London: Ashgate.

Pisani-Ferry, J. (2012) 'The Euro Crisis and the New Impossible Trinity', Bruegel Policy Contribution, Issue 2012/1. http://www.astrid-online.com/Dossier--d1/Studi--ric/Bruegel_pisani-Ferry_Euro-crisis-and-the-new-impossible-trinity.pdf

Royo, S. (2013) 'Portugal in the European union: The limits of convergence', *South European Society and Politics* 18(2): 197–216.

Saint Paul, G. (1996) 'Exploring the political economy of labour market institutions', *Economic Policy* 11(23): 263–315.

Saraceno, C. (1994) 'The ambivalent familism of the Italian Welfare State', *Social Politics* 1(Spring): 60–82.

Stiglitz, J. (2010) '*Freefall: America, Free Markets, and the Sinking of the World Economy*', New York: W.W. Norton.

Tavora, I. (2012) 'The southern European social model: familialism and the high rates of female employment in Portugal', *Journal of European Social Policy* 22(1): 63–76.

Taylor-Gooby, P. (ed.) (2004) *New Risks, New Welfare: The Transformation of the European Welfare State*, Oxford: Oxford University Press.

Treib, O. and Falkner, G. (2004) '*The EU and new social risks: The need for a differentiated evaluation*', paper presented at the 14th Biennial Conference of Europeanists.

YOUTH, FAMILY CHANGE AND WELFARE ARRANGEMENTS

Is the South still so different?[*]

Luis Moreno
Spanish National Research Council, IPP-CCHS-CSIC

Pau Marí-Klose
Department of Psychology and Sociology, University of Zaragoza

ABSTRACT: This paper analyzes the main characteristics and welfare rationale of the Mediterranean typology. Familism, female employment and care are singled out as three representative areas which provide data on the dynamics of continuity and change in the Southern European countries under examination. Particular attention is paid to the increasing female participation in the labour market and the gradual disappearance of the so-called Mediterranean 'superwomen'. The process of female labour activation is already having a great impact in all activities concerned with the type of care traditionally carried out within Mediterranean households. Final remarks stress the need to pay attention in future research to ongoing societal changes which are bound to have knock-on consequences for Southern European welfare as we have known it until now.

Introduction[1]

A paramount mechanism for prompting social change is the succession of generations with different views about the world (Manheim 1928). This basic tenet of social sciences establishes that social change becomes a possibility when members of new cohorts come into 'fresh contact' with

[*] According to Esping–Andersen's ironic reference to the Four Laws of Sociology (1993), 'Everything is different in the South'. The other laws are: (1) Some do, some don't, (3) Nothing ever works in India, and (4) There are no laws in Sociology.

1. This article was drafted within the SOLFCARE project ('*Solidaridad familiar, cambio actitudinal y reforma del Estado de bienestar en España: el familismo en transición*'), under the 'Plan Nacional de I + D + i, Spain' (CSO2011-27494).

the accumulated cultural heritage. Young people have an 'elasticity of mind' that older people have lost. Largely static and slow changing institutions may experience rapid and dramatic transformation as a result of the 'collective impulses' of a new generation predisposed to new modes of thought.

In this paper, we examine the extent to which some of the features that cluster South European countries into a unique and distinctive welfare regime are blurring, prompted by changes in the interface between new attitudes, expectations and practices. Welfare arrangements in South European countries – Greece, Italy, Portugal and Spain – have traditionally been characterised by the central role played by the family and its interpenetration in all areas of welfare production and distribution, particularly as regards income support and care services. A strong household micro-solidarity has provided high levels of self-perceived well-being. Within families the role of women has been pivotal, as they have often cared for children or older relatives at the expense of erratic careers or full withdrawal from the labour market.

Since recent times, the Mediterranean welfare regime, and in particular its capacity to perform as a social 'shock absorber' and a generous supplier of welfare activities in the informal domain, is facing challenges generated by new lifestyles and emerging social needs of young generations. In this new scenario, the various South European countries are caught in the quandary of either maintaining deep-seated cultural arrangements or promoting welfare structuring to accommodate new demands and aspirations. We contend that the pace and scope of social transformations differs across countries, thus increasing the degree of internal variation within the Mediterranean regime.

Characteristics and rationale of Mediterranean welfare

The distinctiveness of the Mediterranean Welfare Model with respect to other macro-areas of Europe has often been highlighted in rich historical and sociological accounts (Sarasa and Moreno 1996; Ferrera 1996; Petmesidou 1996). For a long time, the Mediterranean has been identified as an area where family ties were strong when compared to regions in other parts of Europe. Such differences have deep historical roots, which according to some accounts can be traced back to the Middle Ages. Despite local variations, South Europeans have tended to follow distinctive practices during their life-cycle, such as late emancipation form parental home, frequent co-residence with parents after marriage, or spatial proximity between the homes of the elderly and their offspring. These practices have kept family loyalties strong and have sustained inter-generational micro-solidarities. A child receives support and protection until he or she leaves home for good, normally for marriage, even when providing such support involves the self-sacrifice of parents (especially of mothers, from whom material and sentimental care is generously expected). Grown-up children are also supported at different stages. They can rely on parents for financial support to engage in costly investments (e.g. purchasing a house or setting a business venture), or for assistance in childcare (Reher 1998; Iglesias de Ussel *et al.* 2010). Families in the Mediterranean European societies also protect their younger members from economic and employment downturns, absorbing part of the effects of high unemployment.

Somewhat in return, when parents face transition to old age, children are expected to help. It is common to see grown-up children monitor the health of the parents and paying regular weekly or daily visits to them. When prolonging residential independence is no longer feasible for the elderly, living with their children has been the solution that was taken for granted within the kin group. In Spain it has always been said that the only truly poor person is one who has no family. The intergenerational solidarity is a strong social norm which seldom breaks down. It is shared by the society as a whole and learned at very young ages (Reher 1998).

The cultural and societal relevance of such practices and beliefs has no parallel in Central and Northern Europe, where family ties tend to be much weaker and the capacity of the family to function as a 'shock absorber' is limited. During the late 1990s and early 2000s, some authors have noted that, despite rapid economic and demographic transformations, historical gaps between family systems largely persisted (Jurado and Naldini 1996; Naldini 2003; Gal 2010). Some observers have indicated that the dividing line between strong and weak family systems is reinforced by the religious cleavage between the more 'individualistic' Protestant ethics and the more 'communalistic' Catholic and Orthodox ones (Greeley 1989). In South European societies, both the doctrines of the Catholic and Orthodox churches have traditionally placed heavy emphasis in the importance of marriage, family ties and family responsibilities for the well-being of individuals and the cohesion of social order. The cultural hegemony and influence exercised by both Catholic and Orthodox Churches were mainly responsible for delays in law reforms undertaken in other countries several decades before, such as the recognition of civil marriage, the rights of out-of-wedlock children, divorce laws, or abortion. Religious traditions have also favoured particular gendered models of care provision, where women take on full responsibility for the domestic realm.

Until recently, the strong institutionalisation of marriage in the Mediterranean world accounted for lower divorce and cohabitation rates than those found elsewhere in Europe. In Italy the divorce law was not introduced until 1970, in Portugal until 1975 and in Spain until 1981. In all these countries, 'no fault' divorce was only implemented a few years ago. In this context, women who decided to get divorced (and their children) often faced stigmatisation and economic hardships, which discouraged many others to follow their path. This has had a big impact in the maintenance of the proportion of single parent households at very low levels. In such conditions, single parenthood was usually brought about by the death of one parent (and seldom by divorce or out-of-wedlock birth). When it occurred, extended family networks often intervened to assist 'broken' families whenever needed.

Within households, the role of women has traditionally been pivotal. Women have often cared for children or older relatives at the expense of erratic careers, or full withdrawal from the labour market, especially after the birth of the first child. Even the fewer women participating in the formal labour market were expected to take on alone – or with the help of their mother or other female relatives – domestic and care-giving responsibilities. The male assumption of the 'breadwinner' rhetoric, together with the inclination of many women to maintain full control over the domestic domain, has too often discouraged males to get involved in domestic and care-giving activities. In these circumstances, working mothers have often been driven to hyperactivity. Such 'superwomen' could only undertake demanding professional activities in the labour market if they were prepared to combine them with full unpaid caring work in households (Moreno 2004).

The existence of strong family support networks and the acceptance of care responsibilities by women has significant implications for the manners social risks and needs are dealt with and, hence, upon the structuring and functioning of welfare states. The centrality of the family enables governments to rely on the family to meet the caring needs of their members and to guarantee their basic economic security, thus keeping political demand for public assistance rather low. Solidaristic expectations and resource pooling within the household have also deactivated demands for the de-segmentation of labour markets, where women and young people have traditionally operated as 'outsiders' occupying less desirable jobs than male breadwinners, either in the informal economy, or under short-term contractual arrangements (Andreotti et al. 2001; Karamessini 2008).

As a result of all these practices, beliefs and institutional arrangements, South European welfare has traditionally been shaped in a differential manner from other regimes. Mediterranean countries have generally been characterised by relatively low levels of social expenditure, weak state support for families, and overall limited success in alleviating poverty and overcoming social and economic disparities. Some authors argue that the fundamental joint characteristics of the Mediterranean regime still remain in place (Naldini 2003; Gal 2010). The empirical evidence gathered in this paper cast some doubts upon such a claim. Some of the distinctive features of the Mediterranean model may be changing, prompted by the rapid transformations of the family (at the level of institutions, beliefs and practices) that traditionally upheld the model of welfare arrangements. Crucial for this development is the emergence of new lifestyles and risks embodied in younger cohorts, and policy innovations to deal with them. The combination of risks and policy responses adopted across countries – and also within them – has increased the inner variability in the Mediterranean welfare regime. In the next section, significant changes in family ties, practices and attitudes are examined with relation to female labour participation and the delivery of services and care within households.

Family transitions and societal change

Three areas of observation can be singled out as providing relevant evidence on the dynamics of continuity and change in Western Europe and EU-15: (1) formal familism, (2) female employment, and (3) care.

(1) Formal familism

Family institutions change slowly, but when they do they are likely to prompt broader societal transformations with implications for other domains – cultural, economic, political. Here we pay attention to the structural alteration of the family as an institution and the social attitudes towards new family arrangements in Southern Europe. New types of households (such as single parent, cohabiting couples and same-sex partners) are increasingly present in Southern Europe countries, although they were illegal or stigmatised only a few decades ago.

Southern families are smaller than they used to be. This is the result of the growing numbers of solo households, those with couples and no children (or with only one child) and the decreasing number of households where three or more generations live together. Marriage has been exposed to great change in Southern Europe. Crude marriage rates have declined all over the OECD countries, but this decline has been especially acute in Southern Europe.[2] Portugal and Spain show rates under 4 per 1,000, far below the OECD average of 5 (Table 1). This is noticeable in countries

---

2. The crude marriage rate is the number of marriages formed each year as a ratio to 1000 people. This measure disregards other formal cohabitation contracts and informal partnerships.

TABLE 1. Marriage rates

	Marriage per 1000		
	1998	2009	Change 1998–2009
Greece	5.12	5.25	0.13
Italy	4.92	4.01	− 0.91
Spain	5.21	3.76	− 1.45
Portugal	6.57	3.8	− 2.77
Belgium	4.35	4.01	− 0.34
Germany	5.09	4.62	− 0.47
France	4.64	3.9	− 0.74
Austria	4.91	4.24	− 0.67
Netherlands	5.54	4.36	− 1.18
UK	5.21	4.4	− 0.81
Ireland	5.52	5.17	− 0.35
Sweden	3.57	5.08	1.51
Finland	4.66	5.59	0.93
Denmark	6.55	5.96	− 0.59
Norway	5.27	5.03	− 0.24

Source: OECD Family Database 2011.

where crude marriage rates had traditionally stood above this average. The exception is Greece where this indicator still stands at 5.12, next to the OECD average. South Europeans marry much less, and a decreasing number of them rely on religious ceremonies to consecrate marriage.

Practices such as divorce and cohabitation, that were very uncommon in South European countries, have proliferated lately, especially among younger cohorts. The progress of divorce can be illustrated by the Spanish and Portuguese examples, which reach divorce rates at 2:4 and 2:5, respectively (in year 2008). Divorce rates that traditionally lagged behind those found in Central and Northern European countries stand today clearly above average.

Cohabiting couples are significantly fewer in South European countries when compared with other EU countries. In Greece only 1.7% of people 20 years or older were cohabiting in 2011. In Italy, 2% were in such a cohabitating situation, 3.3% in Spain, and 4.1% in Portugal. In all four countries figures were well below the OECD average (6.8%). But cohabitation has become more frequent among newly formed couples in all four Mediterranean countries. Differences between the young and older groups are remarkable. Cohabitation is becoming the marker for entry into first union for many Greek, Spanish and Portuguese young couples (convergence in Italy is significantly slower). This does not exclude subsequent marriage if partners decide to consolidate they relationship and to have children.

TABLE 2. **Proportion of people who lived with a partner before marriage**

	18–34	35–64	65 and over
Greece	49.3	21.8	5.0
Italy	24.2	14.7	4.7
Spain	45.2	26.9	2.7
Portugal	34.3	18.4	4.9
Belgium	71.1	36.7	14.9
Germany	49.7	46.8	18.5
France	85.4	59.6	18.7
Austria	75	68.8	32.7
Netherlands	69.7	56.9	16.3
UK	69.9	54.9	11.2
Ireland	75.4	36.6	10.2
Sweden	80.2	88.3	48.8
Finland	94	78.3	32.8
Denmark	89.6	90.9	42
Norway	64.5	70.5	25.6

Source: EVS 2008.

Alongside with the rise in cohabitation, there has been a significant increase in non marital childbearing, two developments that are closely related. Spain (where births out-of wedlock have reached 31%) and Portugal (36%) have converged with Central and North European countries, while Greece (5.9%), and to a lesser extent Italy (20.7%) stand clearly behind.

A complementary manner of assessing the strength of the institutional dimension of family life is to examine the development of new values and attitudes regarding family institutions. When asked how important family in their lives is, a large majority of South Europeans invariably consider family relationships very important. Most of them also hold favourable views of marriage, but in this particular case, some noteworthy differences emerge. According to European Value Survey data, in Spain and Portugal the proportion of people who think 'marriage is an outdated institution' comes close to proportions found in Central European countries (Table 3). The gap between generations is larger than in any other country. In Italy and Greece, negative attitudes towards marriage are less common.

Attitudes towards divorce and cohabitation have also changed signifi-cantly. Most South Europeans justify divorce or find cohabitation as perfectly 'normal'. Table 4 shows the percentage of people within the two extreme cohorts (the young and the elderly) that justify divorce in a broad array of circumstances,[3] the proportion who agree that people can live

---

3. Respondents are asked if they justify divorce in a scale, where 1 means never and 10 always. We draw out responses from 8 to 10.

TABLE 3. Marriage is an outdated institution (percentage that agrees)

	1990	2008		
	Total	Total	18–34	65 and over
Greece		20.9	27.5	10.6
Italy	13.5	18.7	21.7	12.7
Spain	15.1	32.4	41.5	14.5
Portugal	23.2	30.8	33.5	14.3
Belgium	22.5	33.9	32.8	29.9
Germany	30	29.2	40.4	11.9
France	29.1	35.2	27.4	35.4
Austria		30.2	39.4	19.3
Netherlands	21.2	27.5	26.7	23
UK	17.6	23.1	27.3	16.1
Ireland	9.9	22.6	23.5	16.5
USA	8			
Australia		17.5		
Sweden	14.1	20.7	24.2	14.8
Finland	12.5	14.9	22	3.5
Denmark	18	13.4	16.8	8.1
Norway	10.1	19.4	22.8	16

Source: EVS 2008.

together without getting married (either agree or strongly agree), and the proportion of people who disagree with the statement, 'long-term relationships are necessary to be happy'. Spain stands out as the country in the Mediterranean cluster where the percentage of people who find divorce and cohabitation acceptable, and of those who do not think long-term relationships are necessary to be happy, is higher. Young cohorts in Spain have clearly developed attitudes that are more similar to those found in Central and Northern European countries than to those in other Mediterranean countries (especially Italy and Greece). This is clearly seen regarding attitudes towards divorce. As much as 58% of Spaniards under 35 years of age express high levels of tolerance towards divorce, a percentage which is only higher in three Nordic countries (Sweden, Finland and Denmark).

Favourable views of cohabitation are found among most young people across the Mediterranean cluster: 91% of Spaniards under 35 agree that 'it is all right to live together without getting married' (68% strongly agree with the statement). In the opposite end, only 25.2% of people aged 65 and older in Spain strongly agree. In other South European countries, gaps between generations are found as well, but are less profound. In the same vein, the gap between generations in the percentage of people who disagree with the statement 'long-term relationships are necessary to be happy' is higher in Spain than in other South European countries. Altogether, South European countries display a significant degree of

TABLE 4. Attitudes toward divorce, cohabitation and log-term relationships, 2008

	Divorce		Cohabitation		Long-term relationships	
	18–34	65 and over	18–34	65 and over	18–34	65 and over
Greece	41.3	19.5	82.6	46.4	2,0	1.4
Italy	23.9	9.8	65.2	33.8	17.5	8
Spain	58.3	27.4	91.2	64.6	35	16
Portugal	34.3	26.7	87.5	67.2	20.6	7.8
Belgium	27.3	13.7	93.8	74.9	41.2	17.3
Germany	46.5	25.7	89.6	61.2	23	11.5
France	46.9	26.2	96.4	83.4	27.9	14.3
Austria	43.2	15.3	81.7	78	26.4	17
Netherlands	43.2	22.4	85.7	82.8	73.3	54.4
UK	30.0	20.4	86.7	64.9	42.1	29.2
Ireland	32.7	13.4	86.8	47.6	39.0	30.6
Sweden	72.4	72.0	93.4	94.1	42.7	38.5
Finland	62	40.9	93.4	66.2	60.9	33.1
Denmark	61.7	50.0	97.3	92.0	56.5	34
Norway	48.7	35.4	92.2	77.0	38.5	25.5

*Divorce: respondents are asked if they justify divorce. 1 Means never, 10 always. We represent people who give values form 8–10.
**Cohabitation: percentage of people who agree with the statement "It's all right to live together without being married".
***Long-term relationships: percentage of people who disagree with the statemen "long term relationships are necessary to be happy".

TABLE 5. Percentage of respondents who disapprove single motherhood

	1981	1990	1999	2008	Var. 1990–2008
Greece			42.2	45.6	
Italy		43.2	40.4	54.8	11.6
Spain	38.1	23.4	17.9	14	− 9.4
Portugal		39.5	50.2	45.4	5.9
Belgium	32.3	34.8	36.5	31	− 3.8
Germany		36.3	31.4	36.4	0.1
France	21.4	26.3	27.5	32.7	6.4
Austria		27.6	25.7	33.4	5.8
Netherlands	42.3	45.5	29	34.1	− 11.4
UK		47.8	38.3	38.7	− 9.1
Ireland		60.8	35.8	28.2	− 32.6
USA	57.8		44.4		
Australia					
Sweden	28.5	46.8	39.9	48.1	1.3
Finland		20.1	26.4	15.3	− 4.8
Denmark		20	36.5	22.7	2.7
Norway	34.1	47.4	52.8	31.1	− 16.3

Source: EVS 2008.

variation in attitudes towards marriage and practices related to the management of couple relationships, with Spaniards clearly standing out as an 'outlier' within the Mediterranean world. Portugal situates somewhere in between the Spanish case and the Italian and Greek cases. Likewise, Spain's young cohorts express least disapproval attitudes towards single motherhood across Europe (Table 5).

A second institutional dimension related to family life which has undergone dramatic changes is childrearing. Children are increasingly scarce in developed industrial societies, often in the same countries with high fertility rates some decades ago. The decline in fertility rates reflects constrains for families who intend to have children, such as uncertain job prospects or difficulties in combining work and family life. But beyond such considerations, having children is no longer seen as a duty or as a cultural imperative to be fulfilled in Southern Europe (Table 6). The percentage of older Italians (65 years and older) who agree with the statement 'It is duty towards society to have children' is 2.8 times higher than among young people (18 to 34 years old), 2.3 times higher in Spain, and 2.2 times in Greece. Similarly, the percentage of people agreeing with the statement 'women need children in order to be fulfilled' varies across age groups: it is 1.95 times higher among older Spaniards than among young ones and 1.8 times higher in Portugal. Young South European families have entered a new scenario, where having children has become more a decision to be taken by the partners involved, rather than being the

TABLE 6. Attitudes toward childrearing

	It is a duty to have children		Women need children to be fulfilled	
	18–34	65 and over	18–34	65 and over
Greece	32.2	69.3	71.7	89
Italy	14.7	38.5	50.5	68.5
Spain	23.6	55	35.4	61.9
Portugal	36.3	57.1	42.4	76.2
Belgium	9.5	31.6	25.8	42.3
Germany	22.9	73.2	41.5	65.2
France	10	43.4	52.6	76
Austria	21.9	34.3	32.8	45.9
Netherlands	1.7	8.3	4.4	12.4
UK	13.4	10.5	15.3	22.5
Ireland	19.5	28.6	15.5	29.4
Sweden	6	6.1	6.8	7.6
Finland	9.7	14.3	6	
Denmark	12	22	72.3	84.6
Norway	13.7	16.2	17.3	14.3

Source: EVS 2008.

result of compelling social norms and cultural expectations. Attitudes among Spaniards seem again to be changing at a faster pace than in other Mediterranean countries, bringing them in line with attitudes found in Central and Northern Europe.

(2) *Female employment*

A major change in the Mediterranean regimen relates to increasing women's participation in the formal labour market (except for Portugal, where female enrolment rates had traditionally been high). This is having important implications for both care and support that families are able to provide to their dependent members, and creates new pressures for balancing work and family responsibilities. The increase in female employment rates has been larger in Spain than in any other Mediterranean country. A close look at labour participation patterns across life-cycles in Table 7 reveals that female employment rates in Spain are similar to those found in Continental Europe and Britain and Ireland for those under 30 years (pre-maternal years for most of them). Such rates are somewhat lower for women on their thirties and early forties (in parallel with child rearing commitments), and they are notably lower in older ages.

Dual-earner families have proliferated in all Mediterranean countries. In countries where young residential emancipation has traditionally been postponed until 'finding' a suitable partner, the availability of two sources

TABLE 7. Female employment rates at different ages

	25–29	35–39	55–59	Maternal gap
Greece	63	65.4	33	− 12.1
Italy	55.1	63	33.8	− 11.1
Spain	72	66.7	38.1	− 11.1
Portugal	72.3	79.4	52.5	− 9.3
Belgium	75	74.1	38.8	− 12.2
France	72.8	76.6	52.4	− 12.7
Germany	68.9	74.3	58.9	− 13.7
Austria	73.9	79.9	42.6	− 12.7
Netherlands	82.1	78.7	54.7	− 6.7
UK	72.9	73.6	63.9	− 13.8
Ireland	78.7	67.4	47.2	− 15
Sweden	75.8	84.4	77.7	2.8
Finland	73.6	79	70.1	− 12.2
Denmark	79.4	84	73.8	− 2.9
Norway	79.1	84.5	73.9	

*Maternal gap: difference between the employment rate of women 25–49 years old and the employment rate of mothers with children under 15.
Source: OECS Employment Database.

of income has become a requirement *sine qua non* for the couple to stand on their own two feet. Dual-earner families have proved to be the best strategy to purchase housing and a good deterrent against poverty in the early stages of the family cycle (Pavolini and Ranci 2008; Iglesias de Ussel *et al.* 2010).

Percentages for all four countries were close to OECD-21 average in 2008 (around 57%) with that of Portugal significantly higher (63%) (EU LFS 2008) A singular feature of many of these new families is that both partners work full time, posing thus severe difficulties for balancing work and care responsibilities in these families (Moreno 2006). Such difficulties are especially notorious for dual-earner couples with children. Approximately, 90% of children in dual-earner couples in Portugal and Greece live in households where both parents work full time. In Spain and Italy, this type of arrangements based in full-time work is significantly lower (around 60%), but still much higher than the proportions found in northern European countries, where part-time work is common in couples with children (especially among women).

Support for the dual earner model is well established in Mediterranean Europe. A large majority of Southern Europeans think that both partners should contribute to household income. More than 90% of the people across Southern Europe either 'agree' or 'strongly agree' with such a statement, a percentage that has not changed significantly since the early nineties. Favourable attitudes have always been strong in Portugal, where, as mentioned above, women employment rates have traditionally been high (Guerreiro *et al.* 2009). In other Mediterranean countries commitment to the dual earner model is stronger today than 20 years ago: the percentage of people that strongly agree with the statement used in the European Value Survey has increased substantially when comparing responses in the 2008 wave with those given in the 1990 survey. The increase has been particularly large in Spain (from 28.4% to 47.9%), where the levels reached in 2008 stand among the highest in Europe (only below Norway and France).

The 'flip side' of these orientations to work among South European is attitudes towards housewifery. About half of Mediterranean women find housewifery as fulfilling as having a paid job. The percentages in Southern Europe are not much different from those in other European countries (with the exception of Britain and Ireland or Finland, where the role is very well regarded). Women in younger cohorts attach low value to housewifery. The gap in attitudes between young and old women is around 30 point in Italy and Spain, and somewhat lower in Greece and Portugal.

Unlike their mothers, a large amount of women in the younger cohorts have attained high education credentials, which feed professional aspirations that are incompatible with taking on the lion's share of domestic and caring responsibilities. Even those who have low education levels have increased their priorities towards a professional career. These labour-oriented women are reluctant to accept 'superwomen' roles, in which they strive to manage 'impossible situations' (Nicole-Drancourt 1989), where they are the main providers of household services for the family while they simultaneously carry on with their professional activities. As a result, care practices have changed substantially.

Not long before, many young couples transferred caring responsibilities to grandparents and older relatives, reinforcing thus the cultural bases of the model of 'family and kin solidarity' in Southern Europe (Naldini 2003). But this strategy has its limits for a number of reasons. First, older *mater familias* available to take on caring roles are decreasing, as they are more prone to stay within the labour market and, thus, have less manoeuvrability to carry out demanding unpaid tasks for their daughters. Second, traditional arrangements display many sub-optimal features that leave family needs and expectations unfulfilled. The most obvious example is the growing gap between real and desired fertility. On average, women in their thirties in Spain, Italy or Greece have given birth to half the number of children that they ideally would like to have. Many will end up having fewer children than they would have wished (Marí-Klose and Marí-Klose 2006). Third, there is growing evidence showing that new 'care deficits' in South European households are being met by new strategies of *commodification* of care work, although still within the limits of the household. Thus, recent studies have gathered evidence indicating that care is moving from the traditional realm of unpaid family support to a grey area of poorly paid work performed mostly by female immigrant workers (Moreno-Fuentes and Bruquetas 2011).

(3) *Personal social services and family care*

The transition of Mediterranean societies to a new scenario where women have reduced their commitment to unpaid tasks in the household, poses challenges for the provision of services and care within the family. A first question that is frequently raised is to what extent men are devoting their time to activities in the domestic sphere, contributing in this manner to meet some of the needs left unfulfilled by the decline of housewives' work. Table 8 reproduces data on the portion of time that women say their partners spend carrying out housework. Figures indicate the percentage of male partners who perform more than 25% of the total time devoted to such activities within the couple (drawn from the European Social Survey, Round 2). In other words, we estimate the proportion of male partners who cooperate significantly in domestic chores, although many of them

TABLE 8. New masculinities in Europe, by age groups

	1. Men who cooperate with their female partners*		2. Attitudes towards male responsibility for home and children**		
	18–44	45 and over	18–34	35–64	65 and over
Greece	9.5	4.9	29.4	31.2	31.1
Italy			36.3	34.8	31.4
Spain	29.9	14.9	60.7	58.9	39.9
Portugal	17	8.8	30.8	25.6	25
Belgium	32.2	32	50.2	52.4	46
Germany	26.6	31.6	70.3	63.1	62.8
France	33.2	24.8	49.9	44.5	42.9
Austria	22.7	29.9	42.5	38	65.6
Netherlands	29.7	29.8	18.2	25.2	21.7
UK	27.8	33.7	39.3	27.2	23.2
Ireland	20	17.8	43.7	37.6	36.4
Sweden	61.1	45	69.9	59.5	58.1
Finland	51.9	51.9	53	49.4	47.2
Denmark	47.2	47.5	62.2	63.8	58.9
Norway	43.5	43.9	80	79.7	77

*Men who take on more than 1/4 of the total housework time (female responses).
**Strong agreement with the statement: Men should take the same responsibility for home and children.
Source: ESS 2004 (1) and EVS 2008 (2).

may spend between 1/4 and half of the time (and therefore still do less than their female partners).

According to figures in Table 8, young Mediterranean males tend to be more 'cooperative' than their older counterparts. The highest proportion of cooperative male partners in Southern Europe is found in Spain. Close to one out of three young males in Spain cooperate with their female partners. Aggregate data across Europe seem to confirm findings of other studies conducted at the individual level. The behaviour of men appears to be affected by the extent to which women are economically independent and hold non-traditional gender expectations (Davis *et al.* 2004; Geist 2005). Countries where women have consolidated their 'bargaining' capacity, as a result of their higher educational levels and better economic resources, tend to score higher in gender equality within the family sphere.

Individual factors do not necessarily account fully for the variance found across countries.[4] As broader normative environments, national contexts matter may contribute to shape the propensity of men to

4. For instance, variation between male cooperation in Portugal, where the level of female labour participation is higher but the proportion of cooperative men is significantly lower.

cooperate. Pressures for women to do and men to avoid housework are likely to be stronger when views supporting a strict division of housework are widespread, as it may be the cases of Greece, Italy and Portugal. In contrast, it may be expected that men will feel more compelled to devote more time and effort to housework in response to widely held attitudes legitimising such behaviours. Normative orientations are found in Spain to a much larger extent than in other Southern European countries, especially among younger cohorts. Similar strong support for male involvement reaches levels only found in France and some Nordic countries. Not surprisingly, the gap between younger and older generations in Spain is the largest.

A second question regarding housework is whether caring responsibilities have been transferred from young working mothers to grandparents – generally women, or 'granny-mothers'– and other relatives. Evidence is far from conclusive, due to limited data available. According to data of the European Social Survey 2004 (Table 9), the hypothesis that South European parents and grandparents are providing services to their grown ups children and grandchildren (living in a different household) to a much larger extent than their counterparts in Central and North European countries is unwarranted.

Childcare responsibilities have increasingly been externalised to formal services, relieving grandparents and other relatives from the need to provide broad support. At this point in time, enrolment rates of children

TABLE 9. Provision of housework and care support for grown up children and grandchildren

	None	Some support	A lot
Greece	59.8	29.9	9.4
Italy			
Spain	72.7	23	3.7
Portugal	56.3	37.8	5.4
Belgium	57.7	33.4	7.5
France	63.5	30	6.4
Germany	58.2	31.4	7.9
Austria	46.3	41.5	9.6
Netherlands	76.3	19.3	3.1
UK	70.3	21	6.7
Ireland	67.4	25	7.1
Sweden	64	30	4.4
Finland	62.5	32.5	2.5
Denmark	67.7	26.1	3
Norway	63.6	29.6	4.4

*people aged 40 and over with grown up children or grandchildren.
Source: ESS 2004.

TABLE 10. Enrolment in formal care for the under 3s and pre-school from 3 to 5 years, 2008

	Under 3 years	3 to 5
Greece	15.7	46.6
Italy	29.2	97.4
Spain	37.5	98.5
Portugal	47.4	79.2
Belgium	48.4	99.4
France	42	99.4
Germany	17.8	92.7
Austria	12.1	77.6
Netherlands	55.9	67.1
UK	40.8	92.7
Ireland	30.8	56.4
Sweden	46.7	91.1
Finland	28.6	74.2
Denmark	65.7	91.5
Norway	51.3	94.5

Source: OECD family database.

aged three to five years in pre-school are nearly universal. Enrolment rates for children under three years have increased dramatically in the last decade. According to OECD data, in Spain the proportion of children of 0–3 years in childcare centres (both public and private) has increased from 5% in 2000 to 37.5% in 2008 (OECD 2001; OECD Family database 2011). In Portugal, the progress is comparable: from 12% in 2000 to 47.4% in 2008. Greece clearly lags behind with just 15.7% of children in formal care under three years, and 46.6% for those of 3.5 years (see Table 10).

A growing number of Mediterranean women have lost the reluctance to enrol their children under six years of age in formal childcare. Social pressures requiring them to devote themselves full time to the care of young children has weakened, although differences across the Mediterranean area are noteworthy. Except Spaniards, a majority of South Europeans think that holding a job for mothers with children under three is detrimental for the latter (Table 11). Attitudes in Italy, Greece and Portugal provide a regime picture (Mediterranean) which is still different from all other welfare clusters (Anglo-Saxon, Continental and Nordic).

On examining attitudes towards care for the elderly, familistic orientations in Southern Europe remain vigorous, despite that needs for care and practices of delivery have dramatically changed. Elders live longer than ever before and, due to improvements in their financial and health status, most of them tend to maintain residential and personal autonomy until they reach very old ages. According to different survey and qualitative studies conducted in Southern Europe, the needs for care that emerge are covered

TABLE 11. Attitudes to mother's work when she has a pre-school child

	1990	1999	2008
Greece	78.2		72.5
Italy	77.8	81.4	75.8
Spain	66.2	45.8	47.7
Portugal	84.2	72.2	65.5
Belgium	60.8		37.4
France	65.4	56.2	38.6
Germany	84.3	73.2	50.2
Austria	82.9		64.6
Netherlands	63.2	45.7	39
UK	54.6	46.2	36.3
Ireland	52.8		33.8
Sweden	73.5	37.8	19.4
Finland	52.4		21.8
Denmark	32	18	8.6
Norway	45.6		19.4

*percentage of people agreeing with the statement:Pre-school child suffers with working mother.
Source: EVS 2008.

informally inside the household by a family member, usually a women that does not receive any regular financial compensation for her work. Mediterranean families show a strong commitment to assist frail elders, whatever it takes. Around 90% of South Europeans agree with the statement 'it's the duty of a child to care for an ill parent'. No significant differences are observed across generations. Such figures stand in sharp contrast with those found in Northern Europe. In general, in Catholic countries (including Belgium and France, and to a lesser extent, Germany, Austria and Ireland), attitudes favouring family involvement in caring activities for the elderly are widespread and intense.

It remains to be seen whether attitudes change as families increasingly externalise care to informal paid workers. The growing use of informal paid work in Southern Europe is a recent phenomenon, made possible by the massive influx of international female workers into countries that had traditionally had low levels of immigration. The new arrangements may not contradict previous orientations and expectations, since the informal work of immigrants is most often still monitored (and often directly paid) by family members. Care is generally considered as a female gendered area within the household, where the employer (usually a women) establishes a personal relationship with the employee and sets the terms under which caring tasks are performed (Lutz 2007). On the other hand, the development of new long term care policies does not necessarily contribute to the institutionalisation of a new professional sector that 'defamilises' care, as found in Northern Europe (Pavolini and Ranci 2008).

A good example is provided by the new Spanish Dependency Law. Despite initial intentions to prioritise the creation of facilities for dependents that would take the place of families (at least partially), the largest part of benefits have become subsidies for family care giving within the household. These moneys often end up being transferred to non-professional external carers (immigrants, in many cases). As a result, attitudes and expectations about care responsibilities may not change as significantly as one would expect under conditions of externalisation of care.

Concluding remarks

It has been argued that the core institutional traits of a welfare regime are extremely unyielding to reform, no matter how pending or necessary such reform may be. This argument may have been overstated. In this paper, we have identified 'collective impulses' that may lead traditional welfare arrangements in directions that were not easy to envisage some years ago. These impulses are related to societal changes, particularly as regards lifestyles and needs of young generations now increasingly clashing with expectations, practices and arrangements characteristic of Mediterranean welfare. The dynamics of continuity and change differ across Southern EU countries. A certain degree of ambivalence remains concerning the 'defamilisation' of care arrangements, as shown in the widening gulf between two distinct sub-groupings: Italy-Greece and Spain-Portugal. With regard to the latter sub-group, Spain appears to stand out as an 'outlier' country which is leaving behind some of the features and rationales that have characterised the South European regime. The available evidence seems to validate the interpretation that a 'Nordic path' had already been taken by the Spanish welfare state (Moreno 2008). However, the impact of the economic crisis raises serious doubts on whether such a path can be followed.

Indeed, South European countries are undergoing financial difficulties that are adding new challenges to the re-structuring of welfare arrange-ments. With high rates of unemployment, young people are facing the brunt of the downturn. The decline of formal familism has weakened the model of family and kin solidarity that has traditionally provided well-being for the most vulnerable members of the household, and very especially for the young. Changes in young female lives have also fostered new individual aspirations that clash with expectations of care widely held by older generations. In a context of serious budget constraints, it is unlikely that governments will have the capacity to expand social protection and to comply with the needs of younger generations in the foreseeable future. If worst comes to worst, young people may be additionally harmed by cuts in a welfare domain already unfriendly to them in areas such as housing, education, family and active labour market policies. Signs of discontent with current arrangements have already been voiced loudly in the streets and major squares of many South European cities.

All things considered, the ingrained conviction of inertia attributed to Mediterranean familism may be challenged. The long-standing claim that the family remains the Alpha and Omega institution shaping all prospective scenarios for Southern European welfare is being shacked by unforeseen 'collective impulses' of a new generation: *Eppur si muove?*

References

Andreotti, A., García, S., Gómez, A., España, P., Kazepov, Y. and Mingione, E. (2001) 'Does a Southern European model exists', *Journal of European Area Studies* 9(1): 43–62.

Davis, S. N., Theodore N. and Greenstein, T. N. (2004) 'Cross-national variations in the division of household labor', *Journal of Marriage and Family* 66: 1260–71.

Esping-Andersen, G. (1993) 'The comparative macro-sociology of welfare states', in L. Moreno (ed.), *Social Exchange and Welfare Development*, Madrid: CSIC, pp. 123–36.

EU-LFS (2010) 'European Union Labour Force Survey (EU LFS) for 2007 and 2008', http://epp.eurostat.ec.europa.eu/portal/page/portal/microdata/lfs.

Ferrera, M. (1996) 'The "Southern Model" of Welfare in Social Europe', *Journal of European Social Policy* 6(1): 17–37.

Gal, J. (2010) 'Is there an extended family of welfare states?', *Journal of European Social Policy* 20(4): 283–300.

Geist, C., (2005) 'The welfare state and the home: Regime differences in the domestic division of labour', *European Sociological Review* 21(1): 23–41.

Greeley, A. M. (1989) *Religious Change in America*, Cambridge, MA: Harvard University Press.

Guerreiro, M. D., Torres, A. and Capucha, L. (eds) (2009) *Welfare and Everyday Life. Portugal in the European Context*, Vol. III, CIES, ISCTE-IUL, Oeiras: Celta Editora.

Iglesias de Ussel, J., Marí-Klose, P., Marí-Klose, M. and González Blasco, P. (2010) *Matrimonios y parejas jóvenes. España 2009*, Madrid: Fundación SM.

Jurado Guerrero, T. and Naldini, M. (1997) 'Is the South so different? Italian and Spanish families in comparative perspective', in M. Rhodes (ed.), *Southern European Welfare States: Between Crisis and Reform*, London: Franck Cass/Routledge, pp. 42–66.

Karamessini, M. (2008) 'Continuity and change in the Southern European Social Model', *International Labour Review* 147(1): 43–70.

Lutz, H. (2007) 'Domestic work', *European Journal of Women's Studies* 14(3): 187–92.

Manheim, K. (1928/1952) 'Das Problem der Generationen', *Kölner Vierteljahreshefte für Soziologie* 7(2): 157–85; 3: 309–30 [English Ed.: 'The Problem of Generations', in P. Kecskemeti (ed.), *Essays on the Sociology of Knowledge by Karl Mannheim*, New York: Routledge & Kegan Paul.

Marí-Klose, P and Marí-Klose, M. (2006) *Edad del cambio. Jóvenes en los circuitos de la solidaridad intergeneracional*, Madrid: Centro de Investigaciones Sociológicas

Marí-Klose, P., Marí-Klose, M., Vaquera, E. and Argeseanu Cunningham, S. (2010) *Infancia y futuro. Nuevas realidades, nuevos retos*, Barcelona: Fundación La Caixa.

Moreno-Fuentes, Francisco Javier y Bruquetas-Callejo, María (2011) *Immigration and the Welfare State in Spain*, Barcelona: La Caixa. http://obrasocial.lacaixa.es/StaticFiles/StaticFiles/670e2a8ee75bf210VgnVCM1000000e8cf10aRCRD/es/vol31_en.pdf

Moreno, L. (2004) 'Spain's transition to new risks: A farewell to 'superwomen', in P. Taylor-Gooby (ed.), *New Risks, New Welfare: The Transformation of the European Welfare State*, Oxford: Oxford University Press, pp. 133–57.

Moreno, L. (2006) 'Le modèle de protection sociale des pays d'Europe du sud: Permanence ou changement?', *Revue française des Affaires sociales* 1: 81–105 [Ed. English: 'The model of social protection in Southern Europe: Enduring characteristics?', *Revue française des Affaires socials* 1: 73–95].

Moreno, L. (2008) 'The Nordic Path of Spain's Mediterranean Welfare', Center for European Studies Working Paper Series #163, Harvard University, http://www.ces.fas.harvard.edu/publications/docs/pdfs/CES_163.pdf.

Naldini, M. (2003) *The Family in the Mediterranean Welfare States*, London: Frank Cass/Routledge.

Nicole-Drancourt, C. (1989) 'Stratégies professionnelles et organisation des familles', *Revue Française de Sociologie* 40(1): 57–79.

OECD (2001) *Employment Outlook, Balancing Work and Family Life: Helping Parents into Paid Employment*, Paris: OECD.

Pavolini, E. and Ranci, C. (2008), 'Restructuring the welfare state: Reforms in long-term care in Western European countries', *Journal of European Social Policy* 18(3): 246–59.

Petmesidou, M. (1996) 'Social protection in Southern Europe: Trends and prospects', *Journal of Area Studies* 9(4): 95–125.

Reher, D. S. (1998) 'Family ties in Western Europe: Persistent contrasts', *Population and Development Review* 24(2): 203–34.

Sarasa, S. and Moreno, L. (eds), (1996) *El Estado del Bienestar en la Europa del Sur*, Madrid: CSIC.

THE MYTH OF MEDITERRANEAN FAMILISM

Family values, family structure and public
preferences for state intervention in care

Ines Calzada
Instituto de Políticas y Bienes Públicos (CSIC), Madrid, Spain
Clem Brooks
Department of Sociology, Indiana University, Bloomington, IN, USA

ABSTRACT: This article seeks to re-open the consensus concerning the
interrelationship between family values and public support for government
versus private family provision. We offer new results from analyses of 2001
data from the International Social Survey Programme for a wide range of
countries and world regions. Refining conventional scholarly wisdom,
Southern European publics' have high levels of traditional family values, but
mainly in contrast to other European countries; familism is also notably
strong in Eastern Europe and several of the English-speaking democracies.
Even more surprising, family values support is strongly and positively
associated with support for public child care provision. We discuss
implications of results for understanding the nature of public attitudes and
familism in cross-national perspective, and the limits of theorizing identifying
family values as the primary cause of welfare state development in Southern
Europe.

1. Introduction[1]

Italy, Spain and other Southern European countries have been seen by
scholars as exemplifying the most traditional model of family in the
developed world. An influential tradition of scholarship points to

1. The authors gratefully acknowledge the help of Rosa Gutiérrez and of three
   anonymous reviewers. This article was written under the framework of the research
   project 'Social policies for the elderly and children: preference formation and welfare
   reform', funded by Fundación CSIC-Caixa.

Mediterranean 'familism' as key to explain the demographic and social policy distinctiveness of Southern Europe (Jurado and Naldini 1997; Reher 1998; Moreno 2002; Bettio *et al.* 2006; Callegaro and Pasini 2008; Gal 2010). There, low fertility and traditional caregiver arrangements coexist with cash-heavy welfare programs and limited service provision for youth and the aged.

Despite the widespread acceptance of Mediterranean familism among scholars, the coming of 'post-modern' family forms and the growing importance of non-family cleavages chafes with the assumed centrality of traditional family values to policy and society in Southern Europe. Moving beyond the Mediterranean rim, the widely debated restructuring and/or policy drift of modern welfare states suggests a second set of developmental processes that may exert pressures complicating the interrelationship between family and welfare institutions.

The presumption of much comparative scholarship is that the national publics of Southern Europe endorse family-based social provision, and that these patterns of attitudes are connected to, and reinforced by, traditional family structures (Reher 1998; Callegaro and Pasini 2008). But is this indeed the case?

In this study, we seek to advance scholarly understanding of familism and the Mediterranean regime with three pointed questions: First, to what extent are patterns of family structure and values connected to ideal-typical regimes? Second, what is the connection between family structures and family values? Third, using support for public child care provisions as an indicator of the legitimacy of modern, service-oriented welfare states, how are attitudes on this issue related to the pattern of family structure/values across countries?

2. Care preferences, familism and welfare regimes

The 1990s witnessed the emergence of a pair of highly influential classifications of welfare regimes, one devised by Gosta Esping-Andersen (1990), the other by Walter Korpi and Joakim Palme (1998) (see also Korpi 2000). Other classifications soon appeared, adding a pair of new regimes to those already defined: the 'Radical' model (Castles and Mitchell 1993), and the 'Southern' model (Leibfried 1992; Ferrera 1996; Bonoli 1997). Of these two, it is the operation of a Southern welfare regime that has elicited the greatest debate and attention among scholars (Rhodes 1996; Moreno 2002; Gal 2010).

The Southern/Mediterranean welfare state is said to be characterized by a fragmented system of income maintenance that combines generous programs (pensions, unemployment) with severely underdeveloped areas (basic security, family and care policies); differentiation from the corporatist traditions in the field of health care (with universal NHS's); and a mix of public and private providers of welfare in which the family constitutes the main insurance for risks not covered by public welfare.

Attesting to the theoretical significance of family institutions, Kohli *et al.* (2008: 170) propose the existence of a North–South gradient, 'with the Scandinavian countries generally having the least traditional family structure, the Mediterranean countries (Spain and Italy more so than Greece) the most traditional one, and the continental countries lying somewhere in-between'. Mediterranean countries have the highest levels of intergenerational cohabitation and spatial proximity of family members; care activities carried out by family members are more time-intensive in the South than in other countries (Attias-Donfut *et al.* 2005, 2008a), and adult children provide personal care to their elders (dressing, bathing, eating) much more frequently than in the Nordic or Continental countries, where professional service providers take on these tasks (Brandt *et al.* 2009).

The intensity of care for family members has, in turn, been cited as a factor explaining why helping people outside of the household is less common in Southern Europe (Croda and González-Chapela 2005; Attias *et al.* 2008). Financial transfers between parents and adult children involve larger sums in Mediterranean countries. The frequency of financial transfers to distant family members is likewise notable (Albertini *et al.* 2007; Attias *et al.* 2008b).

This distinctive coupling of low family service provisions by government with a reliance on private, household-level assistance leads inevitably to questions about the role played by citizens' values in the development of Mediterranean welfare systems, and the additional scenario argue for a causal relationship. Citing differences in time spent caring between Continental and Mediterranean countries, for instance, Reher (1998) posits attitudes to family as being critical. A central explanatory factor behind the Mediterranean welfare state is a belief that family members have the duty to help each other, and that certain tasks pertaining to the family do not belong to national government. As Callegaro and Passini (2008: 200) set forth this line of thinking: 'family ties are stronger in the Mediterranean countries, and they induce adult children to think to formal care as something to avoid as long as family members are able to help their elderly relatives'.

This type of 'natural' family model, although largely discarded by historical research (Gillis 1997), may explain how idealizations of Southern families often parallel fears that public care policies could ultimately erode family solidarity. But the later narrative is not well supported by evidence, which puts into question the explanatory power of family values to understand Mediterranean distinctiveness. Feelings of closeness and affection appear equally strong in Northern and Southern countries, as indicated by the proportion of elderly that feel 'very or extremely close' to their children and are getting along 'very or extremely' well with them (Daatland and Lowenstein 2005). Moreover, perceived social isolation among the elderly is highest in Greece and Portugal, even if cohabitation is much higher there than in the Nordic countries (Ogg 2005).

The willingness to perform caring duties of Mediterranean families also appears open to debate. Saraceno (2004) and Rizzi *et al.* (2008), contend that low fertility rates in Italy and Spain indicate women's growing preference to escape from caregiving roles. Bettio *et al.* (2006: 272) argue that immigration and the availability of cheap labour have transformed the Southern model of family into a 'migrant in the family'.

The assumed interrelationship between citizen attitudes and family-based provision could, in principle, be the product of independently existing preferences or instead an adaptation to the absence of adequate public provision. But whether it operates as cause or effect, the underlying assumption among many scholars is that family solidarity lies at the core of the Mediterranean welfare regime. A strong preference for private, family-based provision over government assistance, and a linkage between such preferences and traditional family arrangements, is the key expectation. It is this expectation that focuses our research in this study.

3. Research questions

We situate family solidarity, family values and care provision preferences within a comparative perspective. The thrust of much past scholarship is that family forms should be closely related to family values. If so, we expect to find a correlation between traditional family forms and family values at the macro level of countries and at the micro-level of individuals.

But the connection between family values, welfare preferences and country-specific contexts may be rife with contingencies. Existing institutions may not necessarily represent the wishes of the majority but instead the group(s) with the power to shape rules (North 2006; see also Korpi 1985). Women, the main care givers in Mediterranean countries, cannot be considered a group with power to question and negotiate institutional designs. If this is the case, the underdevelopment of public care policies may not be related to individuals' preferences for public provision.

Also, the comparative underdevelopment of family policies in the Mediterranean may result from a past combination of traditional family values *and* the availability of family solidarity (extended families that remain close and are willing to help each other). But if the traditional model of extended family is fading, especially in countries like Spain, with the lowest fertility rate in the EU (Kohli *et al.* 2005), the relationship between family values and preferences for public policies may be mediated by the availability of family-based care. Familism should thus depress support for public care policies, but mainly when the individual is situated within an extended family network. Otherwise, family values may be unrelated or even positively related to support for state intervention in this area.

Together, the preceding considerations and lines of theorizing lead to the following questions:

(1) Are family values stronger within Mediterranean countries than in the rest of Europe, and do levels of familism follow the borders of welfare regimes?

(2) Are family values associated with the traditional family model, in which there is frequent contact and a high level of mutual help?

(3) What effect does familism have on individual preferences for public care policies?

(4) Does the effect of values on preferences for public child care depend on the degree of available family support?

4. Data and methods

4.1. Data

We analyze data from the International Social Survey Program's 'Social Relations and Support Systems' survey, fielded in 2001. As far as we know, this is the most recent comparative survey that contains both family solidarity indicators and attitudes to public care programs.

We include data for Australia, Austria, Brazil, Canada, Chile, Cyprus, Czech Republic, Denmark, Finland, France, Germany (samples from East and West collapsed), Hungary, Italy, Japan, Latvia, New Zealand, Norway, Poland, Russia, Slovenia, Spain, Switzerland, United Kingdom (samples from Great Britain and Northern Ireland collapsed) and the USA. This leaves us with data for 32,218 individuals clustered in 24 countries.

Our comparisons go beyond European or even Western borders, helping us to place the Mediterranean regime in broader context. The inclusion of non-European 'liberal' welfare states provides useful points of cross-national reference. Data for East European and South American countries (and also Japan) lend further scope to the analysis.

518

4.2. Dependent variable

As a measure of attitudes to public care policies, we selected an ISSP item that concerns support for state intervention in child-care. The wording of the question is as follows:

> *Q. 'On the whole, do you think it should or should not be the government's responsibility to provide childcare for everyone who wants it?'*
> *Definitely should not be; Probably should not be; Probably should be; Definitely should be.*[2]

4.3. Independent variables: Family solidarity and family values

Guided by the theory of intergenerational solidarity developed by Bengtson and Roberts (1991), we build three measures of family solidarity and one of family values. In this scholarship, six dimensions of solidarity are identified, but the data at hand compel us to focus on four of these: (1) associational solidarity – frequency of intergenerational interaction; (2) functional solidarity – patterns of support or resource sharing; (3) structural solidarity – the availability of family members for interaction; and (4) normative solidarity, i.e., familism – norms or expectations of individual obligations to the family.

4.3.1. Structural solidarity: We build a proxy for the number of adult family members each individual has. The number of brothers and adult children are included as '1' for each person, as well as '1' for mother being alive, and '1' for father being alive. Other family relatives likewise add only '1' for each category. For uncles, cousins, parents-in-law, brothers-in-law and nieces/nephews, one point is added when the interviewee has at least one living relative of each type.

4.3.2. Functional solidarity: The 2001 ISSP contains six items asking respondents about the first and second persons to which they could turn for help in case of illness, financial problems or the experience of depression. The questions are worded as follows:

> *Q. 'First, suppose you had the flu and had to stay in bed for a few days and needed help around the house, with shopping and so on. Who would you turn to first for help?'*
> *Husband, wife, partner; mother; father; daughter; daughter-in-law; son; son-in-law; sister; brother; other blood relative; other in-law relative; close friend;*

---

2. Response categories for the item have been recoded so that higher values indicate higher support.

neighbor; someone you work with; someone at a social services agency; someone you pay to help; someone else; no one.
Q. 'And who would you turn to second if you had the flu and needed help around the house?'

The other four questions are structurally similar, but instead involve the following conditions: *'Now, suppose you needed to borrow a large sum of money'* and *'Now suppose you felt just a bit down or depressed, and you wanted to talk about it'*.

We transform the six items into dummy variables that score '1' when the individual turns to a family member for help, and '0' otherwise. Our indicator of functional solidarity is a weighted sum of the six dummies. It adds one point when the individual turn to a family member for help in the first place, and '0.5' for a second place rating of a family member.

4.3.3. Associational solidarity: Our measure of associational solidarity is based in six 2001 ISSP survey items for the frequency of visits between family members. After recoding all responses categories into 'visits per month'[3] we combine items into an additive scale. This scale indicates the number of times per month that each individual visits or is visited by one family member. We list below question wordings for items.

*Q.2 'Of your adult brothers and sisters, with whom do you have the most contact?'
Q.3 'How often do you see or visit this brother or sister?'
*Q.6 'Of your children aged 18 and older, with whom do you have the most contact?'
Q.7 'How often do you see this son or daughter?'
Q.9 'And now some questions about your father. How often do you see or visit your father?'
Q.11 'And what about your mother? How often do you see or visit her?'

–Daily; At least several times a week; At least once a week; At least once a month; Several times a year; Less often.

Q.14 'Please indicate how often you have been in contact with any of the following types of relatives in the last four weeks'. (a) Uncles or aunts; (b) Cousins; (c) Parents in law; (d) Brothers or sisters in law; (e) Nieces and nephews.

---

3. Recodes for questions 3,7,9 and 11: Lives in the same household = 30 visits per month; Daily = 25 visits per month; At least several times a week = 16 v.p.m.; At least once a week = 6 v.p.m.; At least once a month = 2 v.p.m; Several times a year = 0,5 (6 times a year); Less frequently = 0,2 (2,4 times a year). For question 14: More than twice in last 4 weeks = 4 visits per month; Once or twice in last 4 weeks = 2 visits per month; Not at all in last 4 weeks = 0,3 visits per month (3,6 times per year); No living relative of this type = 0.

—More than twice in last four weeks; once or twice in last four weeks; Not at all in last 4 weeks; I have no living relative of this type.

4.3.4. Family values/familism: Our measure of familism, or family values, is constructed by summing responses to a pair of items with which interviewees can agree or disagree: *'Adult children have a duty to look after their elderly parents'; 'You should take care of yourself and your family first, before helping other people'.* Response options: Agree strongly; Agree; Neither agree nor disagree; Disagree; Disagree strongly. (Response options are coded so that higher values indicate greater support for familism.)

4.4. Control variables

Familism and its expected linkages with family structure/solidarity and public child care preferences may be confounded by additional variables. Principal among these are gender, age, religious participation and household factors. To obtain defensible estimates, we include measures of the latter in our models.

Gender is a binary variable, coded 1 for male and 2 female. Age is a continuous variable, coded in years (it ranges from 15 to 101). Religiosity measures the frequency of attendance at religious services, where response categories are as follows: 6 'Once a week or more'; 5 '2–3 times a month'; 4 'At least once a month'; 3 'Several times a year'; 2 'Less frequently a year'; 1 'Never'. Household composition is measured as follows: 1 'single'; 2 'only adults'; 3 '1 adult + children'; 4 '2 adults + children'; 5 '3 or more adults + children'. Household employment status is measured as follows: 1 'two members working full-time'; 2 'one member working full time, or one member working full time and another one working part-time'; 3 'one or two members working part-time'; 4 'at least one member retired'; 5 'None working nor retired'. This last variable was built to be a proxy of the time available in each family for caring duties.

The former controls have been selected on the grounds of previous literature, which has pointed to welfare attitudes as having two general determinants: 'self-interest' and 'ideology' (Svallfors 1997; Lipsmeyer and Nordstrom 2003). Self-interest refers to the interest an individual has in the maintenance of welfare programs, whilst ideology has to do with moral values, particularly justice beliefs and egalitarianism versus individualism. Gender, age and religiosity reference 'ideology' sources of citizens' attitudes, pointing to socialization processes that may lead to particular understandings of the role of the family. Household employment status and composition approximate 'interest' determinants, referring to existing care needs and resources.

4.5. Methods

In the first step, cluster analysis is used to assess the correspondence between the distribution of family solidarity and welfare regimes, as well as to evaluate the distinctiveness of Mediterranean family patterns. Next, we apply linear multilevel regression models to disentangle the determinants of family values and, especially, to verify the association between these values and objective patterns of family solidarity. Results of multilevel models are confirmed with linear regression models fitted to country-specific samples. Finally, we use linear multilevel models with random slopes to analyze the effect of familism on attitudes to childcare. Ordinal logistic regression models fitted to country-specific data provide us with a confirmation of multilevel models results.

5. Results

5.1. Familism and family solidarity in the Mediterranean and other regions

Our results start by considering the patterning of family relationships and family values across countries and regions. Table 1 presents region-specific means using our three measures of family solidarity, and our single measure of family values. In line with past scholarship, the Mediterranean region has higher levels of both family solidarity and familism in comparison to other established European regional contexts, and also the Liberal (EU countries only) regime type.

But our empirical portrait of the Mediterranean region begins to change when we broaden the comparisons to include Eastern Europe and Western, non-European countries, areas not normally included in previous comparisons. Considering these new comparisons in Table 1, the Mediterranean countries fall from the top position of family solidarity on structural solidarity (the liberal welfare regime has the highest level) *and* family values (the Eastern regime is characterized by higher levels of familism). As regards the associational and functional solidarity, these new comparisons do not dislodge the Mediterranean region as still scoring the highest on these two measures of family solidarity.

Additional comparisons with the South American region and with Japan extend our cross-national understanding. The South American region scores the highest on both structural solidarity and familism across all world regions that we consider. For its part, Japan has higher scores on structural and functional solidarity than the Mediterranean region. When combined with the results of our additional comparisons across European

TABLE 1.   National averages of family solidarity and family values

	Structural solidarity	Associational solidarity	Functional solidarity	Familism
Nordic	7,53	21,48	2,65	7,02
Continental	7,51	26,45	2,86	7,24
Liberal EU	7,82	27,12	2,84	7,36
Liberal (all)	8,47	25,51	2,84	7,41
Mediterranean	7,88	51,76	3,14	7,92
Eastern	7,06	35,99	2,94	8,20
South America	10,26	43,81	2,93	8,78
Japan	8,45	35,20	3,32	7,36
Av. Western Europe	7,67	31,30	2,87	7,37

Nordic: Finland, Norway, Denmark; Continental: France, Germany, Austria; Liberal: UK, Switzerland, Canada, New Zealand, the US; Mediterranean: Spain, Italy, Cyprus; Eastern: Hungary, Czech Republic, Slovenia, Poland, Russia and Latvia; South America: Chile, Brazil; Average Western Europe: Includes only countries included in the Nordic, Continental and Mediterranean models, plus the UK and Switzerland.

and Western, non-European regions, the initial distinctiveness of the Mediterranean region thus recedes considerably.

There is a second finding emerging from these analyses. Results from our measures of family solidarity and family values appear to fit poorly with established classifications of countries based on welfare regimes. Liberal democracies as a whole, for instance, score higher on structural solidarity than Mediterranean countries, and the otherwise disparate regions of Eastern Europe, South America and Japan all tend to have high levels of familism and family solidarity.

Given the preceding findings, it is instructive to proceed further and conduct a 'theory-blind' classification of family solidarity and family values. We use our four measures as aggregation variables (standardized), with countries as units to be clustered. Graph 1 present the resultant cluster structure.

The cluster analysis separates our sample of countries into two groups. The first group includes mainly Continental and Northern Europe, with Australia, New Zealand and Canada as a distinct sub-group, and Finland and Latvia as moderate outliers. The second group is composed of a heterogeneous mix of Eastern and Southern European countries, plus Japan, the USA and Chile. Brazil is the outlier within this dual structure.[4]

Looking at country averages in each of the aggregation variables (results not presented) helps us to understand additional components behind the clustering patterns. Countries with relatively low patterns of

4. This structure remains stable using different linkage methods (within-group, centroids, medians, Ward's). Interval: Euclidean Squared Distance.

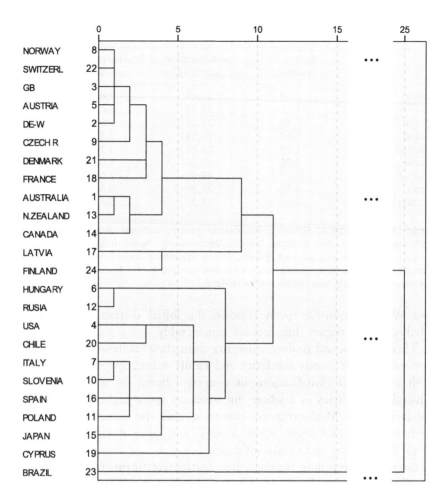

Graph 1. Dendrogram. Between-group linkage. Reescaled cluster distances.

intergenerational solidarity: Continental European nations and Northern Europe, alongside the Anglo-Saxon countries (but not the USA), all have generally low levels of family solidarity. This contrasts with Southern and Eastern Europe, Japan and the United States as regions/countries characterized by much higher levels of family solidarity.

In summarizing these results, the overall fault line separating countries with high versus low levels of familism and family solidarity is not one that corresponds to the existing and most strongly carved out distinctions among welfare regime types. While Mediterranean countries do have higher levels of family solidarity and family values than other Western European countries, our results also show that there are at times larger differences when we bring in non-European nations into the comparison.

5.2. Are family values associated with the traditional family model?

We now turn to the interrelationship between family values and family solidarity, analyzing multilevel models with our measure of family values as dependent variable. In Table 2's estimates, both functional and associational solidarity are positively related with familism, while structural solidarity has negative effects. We estimated OLS models by country with the same variables and these confirm results. Functional solidarity has a significant and positive relation with familism in 16 out of 24 countries. Associational solidarity has a significant and positive relation with familism in 11 countries. In no country do we find negative relationships. OLS models diminish the importance of the negative association between family values and family size for structural solidarity. The relationship is significant only in seven countries, although negative in all cases.

Among individuals, there is clear evidence for an association between familism and two aspects attributed to the traditional family model (high frequency of contacts and use of the family network to deal with risks). However, the size of the family, and possibly the size of the corresponding care burden, constrains in some countries the adoption of family values.

The extension of the traditional family in the country where an individual lives also has an influence on his/her adoption of familistic values, as we can see by the statistical significance of the average of associational solidarity in each country. This indicates that an individual's position within a polity where a large number of families have traditional characteristics tends by itself to increase the level of support for family values.

5.3. What is the effect of familism on preferences for public care policies?

To assess whether familism depresses support for state intervention in child-care policies, we apply multilevel models with support for public child-care as the dependent variable. In Table 3's models, the key finding concerns the positively signed coefficient for familism. This indicates that support for traditional family values does *not* decrease support for public child care. Far from being zero-sum or inversely related, familism and government provision of child care services appear to have significant affinity.

We extend these results by estimating ordinal logistic regressions by country. These results (not shown) reveal that family values have a significant effect on attitudes to public child care in 14 out of 24 countries,

TABLE 2. Linear multilevel models

Dependent var.: Familism	M0	M1	M2	M3	M4	M5
Fixed part						
Sex		− 0,225**	− 0,231**	− 0,231**	− 0,231**	− 0,230**
Age		− 0,002**	0,001	0,001	0,001	0,001
Education		− 0,138***	− 0,136***	− 0,136***	− 0,136***	− 0,136***
Religiosity		0,054***	0,048***	0,048***	0,048***	0,048***
Structural solid			− 0,012***	− 0,012***	− 0,012***	− 0,012***
Functional solid			0,095***	0,095***	0,095***	0,095***
Associational solid			0,003***	0,003***	0,003***	0,003***
Av. Structural sol.				0,100		
Av. Functional sol.					0,232	
Av. Associational sol.						0,030*
Random part						
cons	7,729**	8,370**	7,972**	7,995**	7,975**	8,026**
Var(cons)	0,397	0,364	0,350	0,340	0,346	0,256
Var(Resid)	2,122	2,035	2,017	2,017	2,017	2,017
ICC	0,158	0,152	0,148	0,144	0,147	0,113

N° of groups M0–M5 = 24; N° obs. M0 = 30747; N° obs. M2-5: 27033;

**p < 0.000; *p < 0.05.

Level II variables have been centered to the grand mean (mean of all country averages).

TABLE 3. Linear multilevel models

Dep. Vble.: Support for public Childcare	M0	M1	M2	M3	M4	M5	M6	M7
Fixed part								
Sex		0,074**	0,011**	0,085**	0,085**	0,085**	0,085**	0,083**
Age		− 0,004**	− 0,004**	− 0,004**	− 0,004**	− 0,004**	− 0,004**	− 0,004**
Religiosity		− 0,013**	− 0,013**	− 0,016**	− 0,016**	− 0,016**	− 0,016**	− 0,015**
Household composition. Reference category: household with a single person only.								
Only adults		− 0,001	− 0,010	− 0,009	− 0,008**	− 0,009	′0,008	− 0,011
1 adult + children		0,163**	0,159**	0,162**	0,163*	0,164**	0,163**	0,161**
2 adults + children		0,067*	0,058*	0,057*	0,058	0,059*	0,059*	0,056*
3 adults + children		0,062*	0,050*	0,044	0,044	0,044	0,045	0,041
Household Work Status. Reference category: two full time workers in the household.								
1 full time + 1 full time and 1 part time		0,001	0,000	− 0,001	− 0,001	− 0,001	− 0,002	− 0,002
1 or 2 part times		0,092**	0,093*	0,087*	0,086*	0,087*	0,087*	0,085*
1 or 2 retired		0,080**	0,082**	0,076	0,076**	0,076**	0,076**	0,076**
No adults working/pensioners		0,096**	0,096**	0,085**	0,085**	0,085**	0,085**	0,084**
Structural solid			0,002	0,002	− 0,015	0,002	0,002	0,002
Functional solid			0,005	− 0,002	− 0,002	− 0,001	− 0,027	− 0,002
Associational solid			0,000	0,000	0,000	− 0,003*	0,000	0,000
Familism				0,048**	0,031*	0,035**	0,039**	0,052**
Structur*Familism					0,002*			
Functional*Familism						0,0004*		
Associational*Familism							0,003	
Cons	3,101**	3,099**	3,068	2,710**	2,845**	2,806**	2,779**	2,670**

TABLE 3 (*Continued*)

Dep. Vble.: Support for public Childcare	M0	M1	M2	M3	M4	M5	M6	M7
Random part								
Var(cons)	0,220	0,223	0,223	0,209	0,209	0,209	0,209	0,259
Var(Resid)	0,722	0,723	0,723	0,716	0,716	0,716	0,716	0,713
ICC	0,234	0,236	0,236	0,226	0,226	0,226	0,226	

**p < 0.000; *p < 0.05.

Random slopes Model 7

	Estimate	[95% Conf. Interval]
Var(Familism)	0,002	0,0009 // 0,0038
Cov(Familism, cons)	−0,011	−0,0230 // 0,0014

and when the effect is significant, it is always positive in direction. Consistent with the multilevel results, the ordinal logistic regressions unveil a tendency for familism to possibly increase (and never erode) citizens' demands for public care policies. The results hold if we run country-specific models including alternative measures for education and the number of dependent children (in place of household work status and composition), and also when we use only the item about the caring duties of adult children as indicator of family values.

To assess the scope of our results, we estimated ordinal regression models by country with the same independent and control variables as in Model 3 (Table 3) but now using as a dependent variable an item related to the elderly: *'On the whole, do you think it should or should not be the government's responsibility to provide a decent standard of living for the old?'* The effect of family values on support for state intervention on elderly care is positive and statistically significant in 18 out of 24 countries.

5.4. Is the effect of familism on attitudes to public child care mediated by the availability of family support?

To this point, results for the analyses suggest that support for family values do not depress support for state intervention in child-care even after controlling for the characteristics of the family. However, family values may still shape individual's preferences for child-care policies in ways that depend on the kind of available family support arrangements. Family values may, for instance, increase support for child care policies more strongly when families are small and there are limited possibilities of family-based care provision for dependents.

To evaluate this possibility, we analyze three multilevel models with the same individual variables as in Model 3, but now including an interaction between: (M4) structural solidarity and familism; (M5) functional solidarity and familism; (M6) associational solidarity and familism. Three sets of ordinal logistic regression models by country (one interaction in each set) were also run to firm up results. In these ordinal models we include only variables related to family solidarity and values, excluding controls to see if interactions achieve statistical significance.

Models 4, 5 and 6 (Table 3) show that the effect of family values on support for public child care is not mediated by the extension of the family or by their functionality. The interaction between functional solidarity and familism is not statistically significant in the multilevel models with controls (or in ordinal logistic regression models estimated for specific countries). An interaction between structural solidarity and familism that does reach statistical significance in the multilevel model is due to the existence of a small positive interaction in only two countries: Cyprus and Denmark.

The interaction between associational solidarity and familism is perhaps more interesting as the effect is significant in four countries (Australia, Norway, Czech Republic and Japan). There, we can find a positive interaction between associational solidarity and the effect of family values on support for child care, where family values increase support for public child care as the level of contact with family member's increases. A possible explanation is that contact with family members raises awareness of individuals' needs, and this is translated into increased support for state intervention in care policies. This refines our understanding of the association between familism and government child care support, high-lighting again the unexpectedly positive nature of this relationship.

6. Conclusion

A presumption shared by the large majority of comparative scholarship (and also by regionally oriented theory and research) is that the Mediterranean region is distinctive or 'special' when it comes to the organization and political impacts of family institutions. As we discussed in the introduction, there are several established expectations. Not only do scholars expect to find cross-nationally high or even exceptional levels of support for the traditional family, these support patterns are often thought to be grounded in historically robust patterns of family interaction and dependence. In turn, some authors have seen Mediterranean familism as constraining citizens' willingness to support public service provision, potentially helping to explain comparatively lower levels of welfare state development in Southern Europe.

What, then, do we find when we put to the test expectations of the Mediterranean familism model? Corroborating one initial expectation, family values support is indeed high in the Mediterranean region when we focus on traditional comparisons with Nordic and continental European nations.

But when our cross-national analysis includes more novel comparisons with Eastern Europe, South America and liberal democracies outside of the European region, the picture becomes more complicated. These comparisons quickly lead to substantial recalibration of the phenomenon of Mediterranean familism. We find that high levels of family support and family values in Southern Europe have some important parallels in Eastern Europe and in a number of non-European countries. Moreover, while there are clearly linkages between key dimensions of family solidarity and support for family values, such linkages can be found outside the Mediterranean region as well.

Our analysis of public child care preferences offer a second set of results that put in further perspective theory and research on Mediterranean familism and welfare regimes. Here, we find evidence that the relationship between family values support and attitudes toward government child care provision is decidedly positive in nature. Far from eroding support for public child care services, family values instead appears to increase (or at least be positively associated with) preferences for public provision.

Not only is the Mediterranean regime potentially far less distinctive for its levels of family solidarity and family values than previously thought, the political thrust of familism is toward greater pressure for welfare state development. This offers to scholars an empirically grounded caution against tendencies toward romanticizing low levels of welfare state development in Southern Europe. Far from going hand in hand with one another, there appears to be a disconnection between the policy implications and demands imposed by familism and the low levels of public services provision for families in Mediterranean countries. The current economic crisis and the adoption of cost-containment measures within many countries are likely to widen the gap between family needs and public resources.

In the Mediterranean countries, where cuts in public expenditures endanger the very existence of public care programs, families may be forced to the limit in their role as providers of care and risk protection. Being perhaps accustomed to a lack of public support, Southern European citizens may conceivably accept cuts in care programs with less turmoil or simply more resignation than other nationals. However, the overburdening of families is also likely to be an undesirable situation in the eyes of Mediterranean citizens and, as such, strategies to make the care load manageable are to be expected. Looking at the past, typical strategies include to postpone and limit the number of children; hiring cheap and illegal care workers – generally but not always of migrant origin; and a move to part-time jobs – especially among women. Yet any of these strategies, when generalized, may tend to have negative consequences for future social security budgets and, in all likelihood, with respect to the development of a more modern political economy.

References

Albertini, M., Kohli, M. and Vogel, C. (2007) 'Intergenerational transfers of time and money in European families: Common patterns different regimes?', *Journal of European Social Policy* 17(4): 319–34.

Attias-Donfut, C., Ogg, J. and Wolff, F. C. (2005) 'European patterns of intergenerational financial and time transfers', *European Journal of Ageing* 2: 161–73.

Attias-Donfut, C., Ogg, J. & Wolff, F. C. (2008a) 'Evolution of social support', in A. Börsch-Supan (coord.), *First Results Form the Survey of Health, Ageing and Retirement in Europe (2004–2007): Starting the Longitudinal Dimension*, Mannheim: Mannheim Research Institute for the Economics of Aging, pp. 174–81.

Attias-Donfut, C., Ogg, J. and Wolff, F. C. (2008b) 'Changes in financial transfers: Do family events matter?', in A. Börsch-Supan (coord.), *First Results Form the Survey of Health, Ageing and Retirement in Europe (2004–2007): Starting the Longitudinal Dimension*, Mannheim: Mannheim Research Institute for the Economics of Aging, pp. 182–88.

Bengtson, V. L. and Roberts, E. L. (1991) 'Intergenerational solidarity in aging families: An example of formal theory construction', *Journal of Marriage and Family* 53(4): 856–70.

Bettio, F, Simonazzi, A. and Villa, P. (2006) 'Change in care regimes and female migration: The 'care drain' in the Mediterranean', *Journal of European Social Policy* 16: 271–85.

Bonoli, G. (1997) Classifying welfare states: A two-dimension approach. *Journal of Social Policy* 26: 351–72.

Brandt, M., Haberkern, K. and Szydlik, M. (2009) 'Intergenerational help and care in Europe', *European Sociological Review* 25(5): 585–601.

Callegaro, L. and Pasini, G. (2008) 'Informal care and labour force participation: The economics of family networks', in A. Börsch-Supan (coord.), *First Results Form the Survey of Health, Ageing and Retirement in Europe (2004–2007): Starting the Longitudinal Dimension*, Mannheim: Mannheim Research Institute for the Economics of Aging, pp. 187–203.

Castles, F. G. and Mitchell, D. (1993) 'Worlds of welfare and families of nations', in F. G. Castles (ed.), *Families and Nations: Patterns of Public Policy in Western Democracies*, Dartmouth: Aldershot, pp. 93–128.

Croda, E. and Gonzalez-Chapela, J. (2005) 'How do European older adults use their time?', in A. Börsch-Supan, A. Brugiavini, H. Jürges, J. Mackenbach, J. Siegrist and G. Weber (eds), *Health, Ageing and Retirement in Europe - First Results from the Survey of Health, Ageing and Retirement in Europe*, Mannheim: MEA, pp. 265–92.

Daatland, S. O. and Lowenstein, A. (2005) 'Intergenerational solidarity and the family–welfare state balance', *European Journal of Ageing* 2(3): 174–82.

Esping-Andersen, G. (1990) *The Three Worlds of Welfare Capitalism*, Cambridge: Polity Press.

Ferrera, M. (1996) 'The "Southern" model of welfare in social Europe', *Journal of European Social Policy* 6(1): 17–37.

Gal, J. (2010) 'Is there an extended family of Mediterranean welfare states?', *Journal of European Social Policy* 20: 283–300.

Gillis, J. R. (1997) *A World of their Own Making: Myth, Ritual, and the Quest for Family Values*, Cambridge: Harvard University Press.

Jurado, T. and Naldini, M. (1997) 'Is the South so different? Italian and Spanish families in comparative perspective', in M. Rhodes (ed.), *Southern European Welfare States: Between Crisis and Reform*, London: Franck Cass/Routledge, pp. 42–66.

Kohli, M., Künemund, H. and Lüdicke, J. (2005) 'Family structure, proximity and contact', in A. Börsch-Supan, A. Brugiavini, H. Jürges, J. Mackenbach, J. Siegrist and G. Weber (eds), *Health, Ageing and Retirement in Europe - First Results from the Survey of Health, Ageing and Retirement in Europe*, Mannheim: MEA, pp. 164–71.

Kohli, M., Künemund, H. & Vogel, C. (2008) 'Shrinking families? Marital status, childlessness, and intergenerational relationships', in A. Börsch-Supan (coord.), *First Results Form the Survey of Health, Ageing and Retirement in Europe (2004-2007): Starting the Longitudinal Dimension*, Mannheim: Mannheim Research Institute for the Economics of Aging, pp. 166–73.

Korpi, W. (2000) 'Faces of inequality: Gender, class, and patterns of inequalities in different types of welfare states', en *Social Politics* 7(2): 127–91.

Korpi, W. (1985) 'Power Resource approach vs. action and conflict: On causal explanation in the study of power', en *Sociological Theory: A Semi-annual Journal of the American Sociological Association* 3(2), 31–45.

Korpi, W. and Palme, J. (1998) 'The paradox of redistribution and strategies of equality: Welfare state institutions, inequality and poverty in the western countries', *American Sociological Review* 63: 661–87.

Leibfried, S. (1992) 'Towards a European welfare state?', in C. Pierson and F. G. Castles (eds), *The Welfare State Reader*, Cambridge: Polity Press, pp. 190–207.

Lipsmeyer, C. S. and Nordstrom, T. (2003) 'East versus West: Comparing political attitudes and welfare preferences across European societies', *Journal of European Public Policy* 10: 339–64.

Moreno, L. (2002) 'Bienestar mediterráneo y supermujeres', *Revista Española de Sociología* 2: 41–57.

North, D. C. (2006) *Understanding the Process of Economic Change*, Princeton: Princeton University Press.

Ogg, J. (2005) 'Social exclusion and insecurity among older Europeans: The influence of welfare regimes', *Ageing & Society* 25: 69–90.

Reher, D. (1998) 'Family ties in Western Europe: Persistent contrasts', *Population and Development Review* 24(2): 203–34.

Rhodes, M. (1996) 'Southern European welfare states: Identity, problems and prospects for reform', *South European Society and Politics* 1(3): 1–22.

Rizzi, E., Judd, M., White, M., Bernardi, L. and Kertzer, D. (2008) 'Familistic attitudes, dual burden and fertility intentions in Italy', paper prepared for the Annual Meeting of the Population Association of America, April, New Orleans.

Saraceno, C. (2004) 'The Italian family from the 1960 to the present', *Modern Italy* 9(1): 47–57.

Svallfors, S. (1997) 'Worlds of welfare and attitudes to redistribution: A comparison of eight western nations', *European Sociological Review* 13(3): 283–304.

BRIDGE OVER TROUBLED WATERS

Family, gender and welfare in Portugal in the
European context

Anália Torres
Department of Sociology, ISCSP-UTL, Lisbon, Portugal
Bernardo Coelho
Department of Sociology, CIES-IUL, Lisbon, Portugal
Miguel Cabrita
Department of Sociology, CIES-IUL, Lisbon, Portugal

ABSTRACT: How can we explain that same-sex marriages have been
approved in countries like Portugal (2010) and Spain (2005), where the
majority of the population identifies with the catholic religion, when they are
not recognised in countries with more liberal traditions? Assessing social,
economic and legal changes this paper aims to explain the transformations
on family, gender and public policies in Portugal in the context of the welfare-
state. Two main lines of analysis are pursued.

First, changes in practices, attitudes and laws, such as the approval of gay
marriage in Portugal (2010), are discussed and related to social, economic and
institutional processes. The remarkable fall of catholic marriage in Portugal
and the huge growth of children born out of the wedlock, just in one decade
(2000–2010), are only some of the examples of these transformations.

Secondly, the development of social, family, care and gender equality policies
are analysed in order to put the welfare pathway of change in perspective: from
a late start in the 1970s and 1980s to the expanding coverage, highlighting
welfare-state insufficiencies and limitations as well as, more recently, with
ideological and financial pressures for retrenchment.

Bridges and troubled relations between social practises, values and public
policies are also debated. Our research results are based in data from several
sources, namely, European Social Survey (2004, 2006, 2008, 2010), Eurostat
and National Statistics.

1. Introduction

Does it still make sense to identify Portugal as 'familialistic' when it comes to characterise the country within southern European welfare regimes or even when referring to family and gender relations, practises and attitudes? Or does 'familialism' only apply to certain aspects of the Portuguese social model and social relations but not to others?

First, changes in practices and attitudes regarding family life will be the main focus, concentrating on the nineties of the past century but with special interest on the first decade of the twenty-first century. These changes are assessed using both European Social Survey data from different rounds (2004, 2006 and 2008)[1] and national official statistics.

Secondly, the centre of attention will be specifically drawn on the Portuguese social, family, care and gender equality policies and on the welfare state development up to the present. It is argued that, after a late start and the institutionalisation of a broader social protection system, the last two decades are marked by an expanding coverage and a 'modern' approach to family and gender issues. The impact of these policies, however, is limited by the combination of several factors: underfinancing and financial pressures on welfare provisions, economic and social structural features and the persistence of gender inequalities, namely concerning the combination of paid and unpaid work.

2. Relevant changes in family and marital life

How can we explain that same-sex marriages have been approved in countries like Portugal (2010) and Spain (2005), where the majority of the population identifies with the catholic religion, when they are not recognised in countries with more liberal traditions? And how can we explain that in Portugal the majority approved, through a referendum, the right to abortion at the woman's request (2009)?

One could argue that, for Portugal and also for Spain, these and other measures going in the same direction have been approved by left wing parliaments. But especially some of them were also vehemently opposed by the more conservative parties and movements linked to the Catholic Church. So it could perhaps be expected that, in another political juncture, with right wing majority, these laws could be reverted or change to more conservative terms.

However, other research results seem to point out to the fact that these laws have an important social base of support cutting across different

---

1. For southern European countries, European Social Survey (ESS) data present some comparability limitations because Italy does not participate in the ESS, since 2004, and a similar problem occurs with Greece for the ESS 3rd round (2006).

parties and political forces. This seems to be the obvious conclusion from an analysis of several demographic indicators in Portugal and also in Spain. In fact, they show very rapid changes in representations, values and practices, in certain dimensions of personal and family life that have been analysed already in several studies and through different research results (Torres *et al.* 2008; Guerreiro *et al.* 2009; Wall, Aboim e Leitão, 2010b).

The younger generations, both in Portugal and Spain, strongly approve the idea of not condemning having children and living with an unmarried partner (Torres e Lapa 2010). In the same direction, we identify a trend cross-cutting three different generations strongly supporting the possibility of having children with unmarried partner, in line with other European countries (Tables 1 and 2).

At the same time, the actual practices concerning the issues of marriage, divorce and children have changed dramatically. The Portuguese case is illustrative. The majority of people who marry no longer have church weddings. In 10 years, between 2000 and 2010, Catholic weddings fall down more than 20 percentage points (Figure 1), that is, as much as they did in 30 years (from 86.6% in 1970 to 64.8% in 2000 and 43.1% in 2010). On the other hand, births out of wedlock (Figure 2) also went up as much in 10 years as in the precedent 30 (from 7.3% in 1970 to 22.2% in 2000 and 41.3% in 2010). The crude marriage rate also falls sharply from 9.4%o in 1970 to 6.2% in 2000, then going down to only 3.8%o in 2010 (Figure 3).[2]

TABLE 1. Disapproves not having children and living with someone without being married, per generation (%)

	Disapproves if person chooses not to have children			Disapproves if a person lives with an unmarried partner		
	Bust Generation (15–34)	Boom Generation (35–64)	War Generation (65 +)	Bust Generation (15–34)	Boom Generation (35–64)	War Generation (65 +)
Sweden	6,6	4,7	12,5	3,1	2,8	4,3
Finland	7,9	14,7	27,5	4,9	4,5	20,6
Netherlands	10,1	12,3	21,3	9,7	10,7	17,6
Germany	18,5	20,5	37,2	6,1	7,2	19,8
Uk	9,1	4,7	12,4	10,4	9,9	29,7
Spain	**20,3**	22,2	**41,7**	**5,9**	10,5	**44,3**
Portugal	16,6	23,0	34,1	4,3	11,3	24,9

Source: European Social Survey (2006) in Torres e Lapa (2010).

2. It is interesting to note that first marriages are really falling down considerably, since the crude rate includes all marriages and second or third marriages are still going up (Torres, 2010).

TABLE 2. **Disapproves having children without being married and working fulltime with young children, per generation (%)**

	Disapproves if a person has children with an unmarried partner			Disapproves if a person has a full-time job and the children are younger than 3 years old		
	Bust Generation (15–34)	Boom Generation (35–64)	War Generation (65 +)	Bust Generation (15–34)	Boom Generation (35–64)	War Generation (65 +)
Sweden	6,1	4,4	10,7	15,2	13,1	22,7
Finland	**6,6**	8,6	**27,0**	5,5	6,5	14,2
Netherlands	11,1	13,6	23,8	26,8	29,1	37,0
Germany	12,2	12,9	28,4	24,3	26,7	31,5
UK	11,6	18,0	39,9	14,6	17,6	37,8
Spain	**6,6**	14,1	**47,0**	14,2	15,3	21,6
Portugal	6,4	11,8	21,9	13,1	12,5	14,1

Source: European Social Survey (2006) in Torres e Lapa (2010).

The average age of mothers having their first child also rose as much in 10 as in 30 years (from 24.4 to 26.5 between 1970 and 2000 and to 28.6 in 2009). There has also been a drop in the fertility rate, a rise in the divorce rate and an increase in step-families and single-parent families or those who choose alternative forms of living alone (Guerreiro *et al.* 2009; Torres 2010).

Thus, if anything, the first decade of the twenty-first century has deepened the pace and width of a large scale change. Such a quick transformation in the beginning of the twenty-first century can be

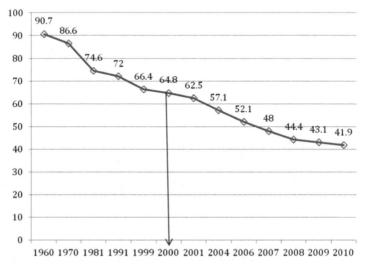

Figure 1. Catholic marriage in Portugal (1960–2010) (%)
Source: Estatisticas Demograficas, INE, 1960–2010.

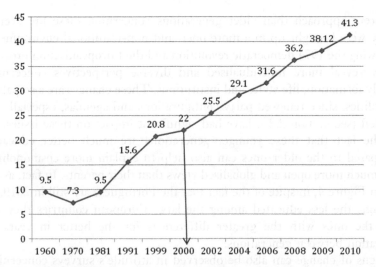

Figure 2. Children born out of the wedlock Portugal (1960–2010) (%)
Source: Estatisticas Demograficas, INE, 1960–2010.

explained, at least partly, by the fact that a younger generation born in the seventies, the eighties and even the nineties of the twentieth century is arriving now at the age of marriage, cohabitating or having children with a

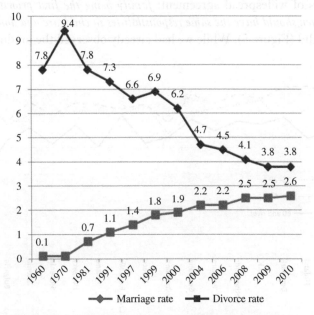

Figure 3. Marriage* and Divorce Rate** in Portugal (1960–2010)%
Source: Estatisticas Demograficas, INE, 1960–2010.
*Crude Marriage rate: Number of marriages/average population.
**Crude Divorce rate: Number of divorces /average population.

different approach than older generations concerning these life events. They were brought up in a more open and non-traditional environment, following the 1974 democratic revolution and the Europeanisation process. They reveal more individualised and diverse perspectives concerning family formation, life styles and institutions. These changes are also patent in politics, since renewed party configurations and agendas, especially on the left (see section 2.2.), have had significant impact on these issues.

The fact that these younger generations are much better educated compared to the older ones can also help to explain more cosmopolitan and much more open and globalised views than their parents. In fact, as we see in Figure 4, in spite of the fact that the Portuguese are still in 2010, in average, the less educated among the large European countries they are also the ones with the greater differences for the better in years of education between generations.

Signs of change can also be observed in attitude's surveys concerning family and gender issues. In line with the general European trend, Portugal, but also Spain and Greece, show rejection of some of the classical and traditional gender stereotypes.

On one hand, the relevance of the family and the role of men in care and domestic life are both highly rated and the ones conveying greater convergence of opinions among all countries in Europe. Two ideas have high levels of widespread agreement: *family being the first priority in live* and that *men should have the same responsibilities in childcare and domestic life as women* did (Figure 5). While we had already observed the predominance

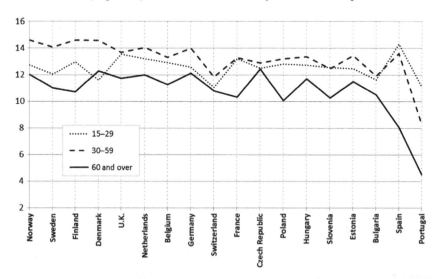

Figure 4. Years of full-time education completed, per age group, per country (2010)
Source: European Social Survey, 2010.

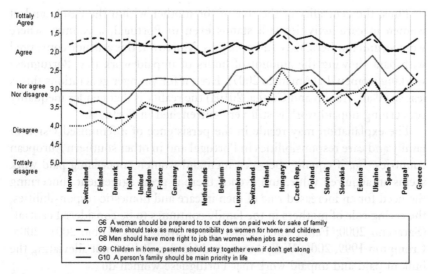

Figure 5. New meanings of the family in Europe (ESS, 2004)
Source: European Social Survey, 2004.

given to family in all countries (Torres *et al.* 2008), the second statement brings, however, some innovation.

Europeans tend to adopt an egalitarian perspective of men and women's roles in the family, and that is also the case for Southern European countries. Undoubtedly, this points out to the erosion of the breadwinner model (Crompton 2006) as a general trend accepted by all Europeans and a 'non-traditionalist' perspective regarding the need for the involvement of men in family daily life and childcare in opposition to the traditional breadwinner role (Sullivan 2004; Wall 2005; Wall, Aboim and Cunha, 2010a).

The topic of equality between men and women concerning paid work also conveys high agreement. The majority of the Europeans reject that *'Men should have more right to a job than women when jobs are scarce.*[3] However, Portugal and other southern and eastern countries seemed to reject it less than others. The answers to the idea of the indissolubility of marriage or relationship due to the existence of children – *Children in home, parents should stay together even if don't get along* – follow almost the same pattern.

The cornerstone showing a clear divide among countries comes when the scenario of the *sacrifice of women's paid job* was at stake *for the sake of the family.* The idea that a woman should sacrifice herself in favour of the family well-being seems to be better tolerated by the majority of the Europeans and only the Nordic countries refuse it clearly.

3. Taking into account all countries in the European Social Survey 2004, 52.9% of the total respondents reject this idea.

Thus, the centrality of the role of the mother within the family and of women in care activities still stands even in Portugal, a country where women, and mothers, have full time jobs. Moreover, this attitude converged with data showing the amount of hours of unpaid work that Portuguese working women do (Amâncio 2007). Even if for younger generations this is less so (Wall, Aboim and Cunha, 2010a) the reality is that gender inequality concerning unpaid work is still very entrenched in Portugal.

The explanation may reside in the persistence of a feminised vision of family and care responsibilities in Portugal and in other southern European countries. So, if equality between men and women concerning paid work seems an acquired value, and even if there is great agreement concerning the need for an increased role of men in care and domestic responsibilities, the caring role of mothers in the family continues to be considered central[4] (Saraceno 2000; Fahey and Spéder 2004; Wall 2005; Tobio 2001, 2005; Crompton 1999, 2006; Wall, Aboim and Cunha, 2010a), not alleviating the bulk of paid and unpaid work that Portuguese women do.

Looking at the whole picture, and to the answers to the five attitudes' questions, the overall portrait shows a trend towards egalitarian gender attitudes and relations at European level. Considering the role of women in the family, however, we observe an European divide. Only Scandinavian countries clearly reject the idea of women sacrificing their paid work for the sake of the family.

Focusing on southern countries, this might be a sign of the persistence of the idea of the fundamental caring role of women in the family but it also reveals different institutional, economic, political and cultural contexts. As a result of the tension between a greater involvement of women in paid work in southern countries, the lack of sufficiently developed policies for the conciliation of family with paid work and a 'familialistic' tradition some authors qualify mainly as 'ambivalent' the attitudes of women and men concerning these topics (Moreno 2010: 97).

Trying to summarise the relevant changes we have been discussing one may reach some paradoxical conclusions. Concerning changes in practices, laws and attitudes – fall of catholic marriage or birth out of the wedlock, etc. – and their large social acceptance, especially by younger generations, it could be argued that traditionalism or 'familialism' does not apply anymore as a correct characterisation of what happens in the country.

Considering other indicators, however, we could conclude differently. On one hand, there are still high numbers of young people still living with their parents and the family is still important as 'social shock absorber' as

---

4. The way this question is phrased *a woman should be prepared to cut down on paid work for sake of family's well-being* can raise interpretation problems: value agreement or pragmatic reasons?

it has been documented (Saraceno 2000; Karamessini 2008). These are signs of the centrality of the family in a role that has not been fully replaced by the welfare state or other institutions, as it happens in Scandinavian countries a trend that could represent the persistent 'familialism'.[5]

On the other hand, however, the idea that family networks still support and replace the lack of other formal support in young households has been contradicted. Research findings show that because of high rates of emigration – and migration within the country to find adequate jobs – considerable number of young families cannot count on grandparent support (Torres and Silva 1999; Torres *et al.* 2001; Wall 2005; Vasconcelos 2005). Many grandparents are simply not there to help on a daily basis; and anyway many are still in the labour market. Thus, the most common situation is that they do it as a complement and not as replacement of childcare facilities (Torres and Silva 1999; Torres *et al.* 2001).

The specific characteristics of the Portuguese decline in fertility illustrate the complexity of the changes undergone. To begin with, unlike many other European countries, women's labour market participation is mostly full-time, not without consequence (Oliveira *et al.* 2012). Plus, the last decade has witnessed a further drop in fertility rates to extremely low levels, arguably due to factors such as the steady rise of the female unemployment rate, alongside general unemployment, and an increasingly dual labour market, with atypical or precarious contracts affecting in particular younger generations (Alves *et al.* 2011). Uncertain life projects and economic insecurity, material and economic constraints, the rising cost of having children and education have also been associated with further delays in fertility decisions (Cunha 2005, 2007; Karamesini 2008).

Portugal witnesses a constrained fertility model defined by a parental project reduced to one child due to the difficulty to fulfil conditions perceived as necessary to structure a children's life: economic stability and time and everyday life management (Fahey and Spéder 2004: 33; Cunha 2005, 2007). Portuguese women are thus caught by the motherhood penalty, which combines gender and economic constraints produced in the interface between work and family: mothers are committed with the normative expectation to engage in intensive mothering, with children above all other activities; but at the same time they must perform accordingly to labour market normative demands about the ideal worker, who would sacrifice all other concerns for work (Correll *et al.* 2007).

---

5. As defined by Karamessini, following Esping-Andersen 1999, familialistic welfare regimes may be identified when and where family plays a central role in welfare provision and 'public policy assumes that households must carry the principal responsibility for their members' welfare' (Karamessini 2008: 44).

So, if the traditional gender stereotypes seem to be rejected we detect for the Portuguese case a very difficult compromise between the role of mothers in the family and at the same time the full acceptance of equality with men concerning paid work, at the cost of serious inequalities. Rather than 'familialism', it seems more adequate to talk about 'ambivalence' and 'inequality' concerning gender roles in the family, as mentioned above.

Since these processes of change and continuity are still operating and complex, rather than classifying Portugal, or other southern European countries, in the 'familialistic' group or to reject in block this characterisation, what fits and what does not fit in the picture should be subject to careful analysis.

3. Welfare pathways of change

3.1. 'Structural convergence' with Europe in difficult times

How have policy arrangements' responded to these changes? And, more broadly, how do these changes fit into the historical trajectory of relatively recent Welfare-states?

Southern European countries are often located on under-developed conservative and generally 'disadvantaged' welfare regimes (Esping-Andersen 1990, 1999), leading many authors to speak of a 'southern Europe' model, even if many of its characteristics are not entirely shared (Ferrera 1996; Ferrera *et al.* 2000; Silva 2002; Karamessini 2008).[6]

These countries tend to be perceived as being driven by a gender inequality ideology and traditional family and gender structures, placing the main onus of childcare and caring for elderly on family support networks and, particularly, on women. However, a rising number of women in paid work in southern countries as well as broader formal childcare coverage has been witnessed (Karamessini 2008). And, in Portugal, labour market has displayed comparatively high employment rates and a massive full-time participation of women since the 1970s, providing specific elements that hardly fit 'Southern European' label.[7] Plus, family life and configurations have themselves changed, even while equality in access to paid work contrasts in the persisting overburden of women in unpaid work. At the same time, and especially since 1995, while

---

6. For a comprehensive discussion of many different typologies used in comparative welfare studies, see Arcanjo 2006.
7. To the point of leading some authors to question where to include the Portuguese case (Pedroso 2007). Other authors also note, besides important specific features in the labour market, less fragmentation in social protection along occupational lines and differences in social services coverage (Flaquer 2000).

some limitations lingered, policy designs have been much more concerned with reconciling work and family issues, childcare and even gender equality.

By assessing and analysing policy pathways of change in the late twentieth century and in the beginning of the millennium we can draw a different picture: (i) the late start of a comprehensive welfare-state allowed, at least in Portugal and Spain, for the introduction of policy designs concerned with work-family balance policies and gender equality, with arguably less rigid and constraining 'path-dependence' effects (Pierson 2000; Pierson 2002; Pierson and Scockpol 2002) in adapting to cultural and gender-balance changes, with the policy-shaping forged in not fully consolidated institutional and policy architectures; (ii) welfare-state limitations persist but they are more the effect of underfinancing constraints of an immature welfare state system and of a restrictive economic context of 'permanent austerity' (Pierson 2002) than of traditionalist or 'familialistic' policy makers perspectives; (iii) the effect of these limitations has been the persistence of some aspects of 'familialism' and gender inequality not so much as an ideology but as a reality resulting from the combination of Portuguese women combining long hours dedicated to paid work with most of the unpaid care responsibilities.

Looking back, after the gale of new social rights after the 1974 revolution, under democracy and Europeanisation an expanding social protection system gradually took form and became institutionalised. New agendas and a new generation of social policies renewed this thrust from 1995 on, under centre-left social-democrats (PS) governments.[8]

However, the late development of welfare was not without consequence. In the long-term, it has resulted in a double structural pressure of contradictory forces (for a similar argument, see Ferrera *et al.* 2000: 46–8). On one hand, the needs and expectations of welfare expansion boosted by democracy and Europeanisation pushed for the expansion of social rights, higher levels of social protection and wider coverage of social risks. On the other hand, the economic and ideological context dramatically changed since the 1970s. The golden era of economic and welfare expansion gave way to the end of the 'orthodox consensus' around the welfare-state and an era of market-oriented ideological dominance and widespread 'permanent austerity' (Pierson 1994, 2000) with low economic growth and budgetary pressures began – a situation that the global crisis of 2008 – on has only heightened. Therefore, as Ferrera (2010: 618) correctly underlines, this 'late and compressed' modernisation has been especially 'difficult'.

---

8. From 1995 to 2011, only between 2002 and 2005 a centre-right coalition has been in power. The same parties returned to office in 2011.

Thus, pressures for more market–oriented policies have become more prominent, clashing with the expectations towards improved coverage of different social risks. Policy instability and political strife over key welfare areas became more visible, with reforms and often counter-reforms taking place,[9] even if path–dependence effects and the well studied and documented obstacles to welfare retrenchment (Pierson 1994; Levy 2010) have prevented radical changes. Specially in the last decade, these trends are clear. Following the 2008 crisis, the near-collapse of public finances has been a further step to sharpen them.

Despite the structural trend of an expansion of social protection systems, significant imbalances and weaknesses are patent. For example, the protection of old age became stronger than that of childhood or youth (see Table 3) and transfers such as family benefits, despite high coverage and rising amounts, remained relatively low when compared to other countries (Bradshaw and Finch 2002Bradshaw and Finch 2010); and access to the expanded network of care services does not go without the payment of monthly fees by families, in very significant amounts – even in the so–called 'social sector', where NGOs which own and run care services are in many cases highly subsidised by the State. In fact, the under-financing of social services, common to other Southern European countries (Karamessini 2008: 47) is not only a matter of coverage; in Portugal it is visible in its cost for families as pointed out clearly when comparing European countries concerning cost of childcare to parents (Lewis 2009: 93).

More recently, the huge financial constraints that followed the 2008 financial crisis and eventually led to an Euro-area and IMF international

TABLE 3. Enrolment in formal care for the under 3s and pre-school from 3 to 5 years (%), Portugal. 2008

	Enrolment in formal care for the under 3s and pre-school from 3 to 5 years (%)			Expected years in education for 3 to 5 year olds		
	Under 3 years	3 years	4 years	5 years	3 to 5 years	3 to 5 years
Portugal	47,4	63,0	81,3	92,6	79,2	2,4
OECD	30,1	59,7	80,0	91,8	77,3	2,3
EU 27	28,2	68,8	85,6	91,1	81,8	2,5

Source: OECD Family Database.

9. Detailed discussions of different examples, can be found in Silva (2012) for health reforms, in Silva and Pereira (2012) for the unemployment scheme or Dornelas and Silva (2012) for labour market regulation.

support have been at the core of the political agenda. And while welfare reform has been pushed forward for budgetary reasons, ideological issues also seem to be entangled in financial arguments.

This being the overall context, what is interesting is that these changes and tensions seem to not have affected the structural trend of advancement in family policies and gender issues. Apart from cost-containment measures in family benefits to re-focus them on lower income families, other elements of these policies have barely been touched. Therefore, it is important to take a detailed look at these issues to have a full grasp of the width and depth of the transformations that have occurred.

3.2. Family and gender policies

As the welfare-state gradually expanded and matured throughout the 1980s and 1990s, even under oscillating economic performances, so did family and gender issues evolve with a gradual enlargement of social rights and services.

The already mentioned 1995 political cycle change that paved the way for longer periods of centre-left governments seems to have been a decisive factor. Plus, increased political competition between left wing parties may have also played an important role. From the late 1990s and early 2000s on, BE (Bloco de Esquerda, left of the social-democrat PS) emerged as a platform of smaller parties and gained considerable weight in Parliament, thus bringing fierce competition both to PS and PCP (Partido Comunista Português), an orthodox-minded communist party more focused on economic and labour issues. This reconfiguration favoured the renewal of the agenda and a coalition to support it: in women rights and gender issues the initiatives and votes of these three parties were the base for the new laws approved.

Besides an expansion of social benefits, namely family leaves and family allowances (Guillén *et al.* 2001), a gradual enlargement of family services for older people, children, and people with disability began, resulting in a much higher coverage of family services when the departure point was truly negligible. Concerning pre-school children, for instance (see Table 4), at present pre-primary school for those aged five has nearly universal coverage and kindergarten coverage has already met the Barcelona target for childcare of 33% (see, for instance, European Commission 2008; Plantenga and Remery 2009).

Also, the public education system has not only expanded its pre-school capacity to almost universal figures (for those age 5) but it now includes a program called 'full-time school' that has proven helpful in reconciling family responsibilities and working life by expanding the activities and

TABLE 4. Social expenditure with old age and family as% of GDP (2007)

		Cash	Services	Tax breaks	Total
Family	Portugal	0,71	0,44	0,17	1,32
	OECD	1,22	0,78	0,25	2,20
Old Age and Survivors	Portugal	10,8	0,1	-	10,8
	OECD	7,0	0,0	-	7,4

Source: OECD, Social Expenditure Database.

time length children can remain at school.[10] In fact, the Constitution itself included from 2004 the role of the State in the promotion of reconciling work and family life (art. 11°).

The duration of family leaves has been substantially increased for both women and men throughout these decades. As late as 2009, a new reform established that, on top of a compulsory initial parental leave for fathers and mothers, the maximum duration of the subsidy, up to six months, can be granted only if both parents take up leaves, thus favouring gender equality in childcare.[11]

At the same time, a number of important shortcomings do linger. The level of financial benefits remained comparatively low. Family benefits have been reformed from universalism to means-testing conditions to focus on lower income families from 2010 on, still under a centre-left government under enormous public finance pressures. Plus, while, as mentioned, there has been a very significant expansion of the social services networks (for the elderly, children, people with disability), which started from negligible figures to the current levels, many social services are private or ran by NGOs. Even in the latter case, these services, despite being highly subsidised by the State both in construction and operation itself, are often costly to families, thus limiting its accessibility.

Apart from family policies, gender issues continued to undergo vast and profound changes, which seem to have expanded and accelerated in the last decade, and especially between 2005 and 2011, with centre-left majorities in parliament and seemingly with a relevant influence from similar developments in Spain. In Portugal, this period witnessed the introduction of a 'quota' system for women in electoral lists (2007), the law on medically assisted reproduction (2006),[12] a more liberal abortion law

---

10. Executive decision of the Ministry of Education: Despacho 12591/2006, of 16 June. Available online here: http://legislacao.min-edu.pt/np4/145.
11. Law 7/2009, of 12 February, and a more specific decree law: DL 91/2009, of 9 April.
12. Law 32/2006, of 26 July.

following a referendum (2007), a liberal divorce law (2008),[13] more rights to people not formerly married in common-law marriages (2010),[14] deepening the legal recognition of cohabitation relationships outside marriage itself first introduced in 2001.[15] Also, domestic violence became a public offence in the Penal Code revision of 2000.[16]

Plus, gay rights have also been enlarged, first with the recognition of homosexual couples not formally married (2001) and then with the legal permission of marriages between people of the same sex (2010).[17] A more liberal approach to gender identity issues such as sex and name change in a Gender Identity Law was also passed in parliament (2011).[18] The Constitution itself was changed: in 2004, it was amended to include 'sexual orientation' in its rather extensive list of anti-discriminatory safeguard criteria.[19]

To explain this 'second wave' of gender legal changes a number of factors can be pointed out. On top of the already mentioned party renewal and reconfiguration of the left-wing political space, and the arguably diminishing influence of the Catholic Church and conservative social sectors on the whole, the well-succeeded liberal moral and gender agenda pushed forward by the Socialist government of Zapatero in Spain, Portugal's only neighbour and a traditionally conservative country in family and gender issues, undoubtedly played an important role.

In short, gradual but extensive and pervasive change regarding family, work-family and gender policies has taken place. The evolution of women's status, of childcare and gender issues broadly underline this transformation. The modernisation of laws, policies and social and economic structures has been substantive and sustained. Inevitably, it has also been gradual and coexisting with more traditional elements, not least in family and gender issues, as well as insufficiencies and under-financing of services (Meulders *et al.* 2007; Karamessini 2008). Plus, an ambivalence and tension between equality ideas with some echoes of

---

13. Law 61/2008, of 31 October (free access online at www.dre.pt)
14. Law 23/2010, 30 August.
15. Law 7/2001, of 11 May.
16. Law 59/2007, of 4 September.
17. Law approved in parliament: Lei 9/2010, of 31 May (free access online at www.dre.pt).
18. Lei 7/2011, of 17 February. Already under a centre-right majority, this law was passed with votes from the parliamentary left (PS, PCP, BE), plus 7 votes and 10 abstentions from the right. The Constitutional amendment of 2004 (see text) was important, since the right-wing President of the Republic promulged the law invoking 'constitutional imperatives'.
19. Article 4°, n°2 of the Constitution of the Portuguese Republic.

traditional balances and the conditions to practice them is patent (Moreno Minguez 2010).

In this framework, and adding to the already mentioned obstacles to radical welfare change and retrenchment common to other countries, structural elements specific to the Portuguese case (above all, full-time participation of women in the labour market and family changes) seem to provide solid grounds for making changes difficultly reversible (in line with Daly's (2010: 147–8) assessment). On the other hand, tensions and imbalances resulting from the difficult match between social and economic transformations and a late catching-up process are not solved. These tensions are visible in the women's overburden resulting from reconciling full-time working hours and unpaid work responsibilities or in the long declining very low fertility rates.

4. Final remarks

Analysing changes concerning family and gender practices and attitudes taking place in Portugal, in the European context, the paper discussed the need for a more comprehensive approach if one wants to be able to specify what change and continuity really mean. We argue for the need to go beyond classifications like 'traditionalism' or 'familialism', given that special arrangements and combinations between practices, attitudes, institutional and social structural constraints have to be taken into account.

The evolution of demographic data from the last 50 years and, especially, from the last decade, challenges 'traditionalist' assumptions. The majority of the Portuguese no longer chooses Catholic marriage. First marriages also dropped significantly, helping to explain the vertiginous rise of births out of the wedlock; divorce rates are very high even though divorcees tend to remarry and remarriage has continued to grow. From 2006 until 2010 we also identified considerable law changes regarding family, gender and equality issues defying established common sense about Portugal as a catholic southern country. The approval of same sex marriages was only one of the most emblematic examples.

To explain these transformations and their wide social acceptance we argued that their main agents were a generation born in the 1970s and 1980s, considerably more educated than their parents, with more liberal views concerning these private matters; a favourable political juncture and the convergence of a left majority in the Portuguese parliament approving these new laws was another key factor to be considered.

However, a non-traditionalist perspective coexists with the persistence of the centrality of the role of the mother in unpaid work. Thus, even if in the plan of ideals and expectations gender equality is highly rated, in practise, overburden is the daily reality of many Portuguese women mainly working in full time jobs and, especially, mothers of young children.

Some of these findings converge with others concerning southern countries showing that in spite of very clear advances concerning women's paid work (Karemissini 2008: 62) and attitudes clearly pointing out towards equality between men and women, there are still several institutional constraints resulting in 'ambivalence' and 'moral dilemmas' concerning women's role in the balance between family and work (Moreno 2010: 97).

Looking at the welfare-state pathway in Portugal, as other South European countries a latecomer, and pointing out its remaining limitations, we also underlined structural and pervasive changes concerning a wide range of laws and policies, especially visible in the last 15 years. Family-work balance and gender equality laws, in leaves and specifically the development of childcare services, as well as a more general new wave of gender rights (the latter from 2005 on), considerably changed the scenario of a country with a traditional image concerning family and gender issues.

However, the immensity of the country welfare catching-up and its institutional and financial limitations have perhaps contributed to the persistence of some characteristics that can be still associated to 'familialism', if not ideologically as such, at least in the sense of families still having to play a relevant role in welfare provision. Plus, in the current family structures and practices, since 'families' have themselves changed profoundly, this also implies important strains in the management of daily lives and specifically, as stressed before, inequalities between men and women, namely in unpaid work.

Nevertheless, we argue it would be blind vision to ignore the available data showing both (1) long-term huge transformations in welfare, and specifically in family and gender policies, and also that (2) changes concerning practises and attitudes towards family constitution and family relations changed considerably fast and are now far from the traditional image. Moreover, transversal generational effects in values and attitudes among younger generations seem much broader than the political and ideological majorities that approved many of the law and policy changes observed. Therefore, even if welfare faces strong financial pressures, a backlash in a less favourable political juncture would be unlikely. This is precisely due to a modernised symbolic and cultural environment but also to structural factors such as the massive full-time participation of women in the labour market.

References

Alves, Nuno de Almeida, Cantante, F., Baptista, I. and Carmo, R. (2011) *Jovens em Transições Precárias: Trabalho, Quotidiano e Futuro*, Lisboa: Mundos Sociais.

Amâncio, Lígia (2007) Género e divisão do trabalho doméstico – o caso português em perspectiva. in *Família e Género em Portugal e na Europa*, org. Wall, Karin e Amâncio, Lígia, 181–108, Lisboa, Imprensa das Ciências Sociais.

Arcanjo, M. (2006) 'Ideal (and real) types of Welfare State', Lisbon: ISEG-UTL, Working Papers, WP 06/2006, 1–34, http://www.iseg.utl.pt/departamentos/economia/wp/wp062006decisep.pdf.

Bradshaw, J. and Finch, N. (2002) 'A comparison of family benefit packages: A comparison of 22 countries', Department of Work and Pensions Research Reports, 174, Department of Work and Pensions, UK, http://research.dwp.gov.uk/asd/asd5/174summ.pdf.

Bradshaw, J. and Finch, N. (2010) 'Family benefits and services', in F. Castles, S. Leibfried, J. Lewis, H. Obinger and C. Pierson (eds), *The Oxford Handbook of the Welfare State*, Oxford: Oxford University Press, pp. 463–78.

Correll, S. J., Benard, S. and Paik, I. (2007) 'Getting a job: Is there a motherhood penalty?', *American Journal of Sociology* 112(5): 1297–338.

Crompton, R. (1999) *Restructuring Gender Relations and Employment: The Decline of the Male Breadwinner*, Oxford: Oxford University Press.

Crompton, R. (2006) *Employment and the Family: The Reconfiguration of the Work and Family Life in Contemporary Societies*, Cambridge: Cambridge University Press.

Cunha, V. (2005) 'A Fecundidade das Famílias', in K. Wall (ed.), *Famílias em Portugal - Percursos, Interacções, Redes Sociais*, Lisboa: Imprensa de Ciências Sociais, pp. 395–464.

Cunha, V. (2007) *O Lugar dos Filhos: Ideais, Práticas e Significados*, Lisboa: Imprensa de Ciências Sociais.

Daly, M. (2010) 'Families versus state and market', in F. Castles, S. Leibfried, J. Lewis, H. Obinger and C. Pierson (eds), *The Oxford Handbook of the Welfare State*, Oxford: Oxford University Press, pp. 139–51.

Dornelas, António and Silva, Mariana Vieira da (2012) 'Políticas públicas de regulação do mercado de trabalho', in Maria de Lurdes Rodrigues and Pedro Adão e Rodrigues (coords.), Imprensa Nacional Casa da Moeda (ed.), *Políticas Públicas em Portugal*, Lisboa: Imprensa Nacional Casa da Moeda, pp. 155–166.

Esping-Andersen, G. (1990) *The Three Worlds of Welfare Capitalism*, Cambridge: Polity Press.

Esping-Andersen, G. (1999) *Social Foundations of Post-Industrial Economies*, Oxford: Oxford University Press.

European Commission (2008) 'Implementation of the Barcelona objectives concerning childcare facilities for pre-school-age children', Commission staff working document, accompanying document to the Report from the Commission to the European Parliament, the Council, the European Economic and Social Committee and the Committee of Regions, COM(2008) 598, Brussels, European Commission.

Fahey, T. and Spéder, Z. (2004) *Fertility and Family Issues in an Enlarged Europe*, Luxembourg: Office for Official Publications of the European Communities, European Foundation for the Improvement of Living and Working Conditions.

Ferrera, M. (1996) 'The "Southern model" of welfare in social Europe', *Journal of European Social Policy* 6(1): 17–37.

Ferrera, M. (2010), 'The South European countries', in F. Castles, S. Leibfried, J. Lewis, H. Obinger and C. Pierson (eds), *The Oxford Handbook of the Welfare State*, Oxford: Oxford University Press, pp. 616–29.

Ferrera, M., Hemerijck, A. and Rhodes, M. (2000) *The Future of Social Europe: Recasting work and Welfare in the New Economy*, Lisbon: Celta Editora.

Flaquer, L. (2000) 'Family policy and welfare state in Southern Europe', WP n° 185, Barcelona: Institut de Ciències Politiques i Socials, http://www.recercat.net/bitstream/2072/1280/1/ICPS185.pdf.

Guerreiro, M. D., Torres, A. and Lobo, C. (2009) 'Changing families: Configurations, values and recomposition processes', in M. Guerreiro, A. Torres and L. Capucha (eds), *Welfare and Everyday Life*, (Portugal in the European Context, vol. III), CIES, ISCTE-IUL, Lisbon: Celta Editora, pp. 7–35. (I)

Guillén, A., Alvarez, S. and Silva, Pedro Adão e (2001) 'Redesigning the Spanish and Portuguese Welfare States: The Impact of Accession into the European Union', University of Harvard, Center for European Studies, Working Paper No. 85, http://www.ces.fas.harvard.edu/publications/docs/pdfs/guillen.pdf.

Karamessini, M. (2008) 'Continuity and change in the southern European social model', *International Labour Review* 147(1): 43–70.

Levy, J. D. (2010) 'Welfare retrenchment', in F. Castles, S. Leibfried, J. Lewis, H. Obinger and C. Pierson (eds), *The Oxford Handbook of the Welfare State*, Oxford: Oxford University Press, pp. 552–68.

Lewis, J. (2009) *Work-Family Balance, Gender and Policy*, Cheltenham, UK: Edward Elgar.

Meulders, Danièle, Plasman, Robert, Heneau, Jérôme de, Maron, Leila, O'Dorchai, Sile (2007) Trabalho e maternidade na Europa, condições de trabalho e políticas públicas, in *Cadernos de Pesquisa* 37: 611–40.

Moreno Mínguez, A. (2010) 'Family and gender roles in Spain from a comparative perspective', *European Societies* 12(1): 85–112.

Oliveira, I., Gomes, C. S., Pinto, M. L. and Cabrita, M. (2012) 'Fertility, childcare and female employment in Europe', CIES-IUL Working Papers, WP 125/2012, http://www.cies.iscte.pt/wp.jsp.

Pierson, P. (1994) *Dismantling the Welfare State? Reagan, Thatcher and the Politics of Retrenchment*, Cambridge: Cambridge University Press.

Pierson, P. (2000) 'Increasing returns, path dependence, and the study of politics', *American Political Science Review* 94(2): 251–67.

Pierson, P. (2002) 'Coping with permanent austerity: Welfare state restructuring in affluent democracy', *Revue Française de Sociologie* 43(2): 369–402.

Pierson, P. and Skocpol, T. (2002) 'Historical institutionalism in contemporary political science', in I. Katznelson and H. V. Milner (eds), *Political Science: State of the Discipline*, New York: W.W. Norton, pp. 693–721.

Plantenga, J. and Remery, C. (2009) *The Provision of Childcare Services: A Comparative Review of 30 European Countries*, European Commission's Expert Group on Gender and Employment Issues (EGGE), Brussels, European Commission.

Saraceno, C. (2000) 'Gender policies: Family obligations and social Policies in Europe', in T. Boje and A. Leira (eds), *Gender, Welfare State and the Market: Towards a New Division of Labour*, London and New York: Routledge, pp. 122–145.

Silva, Mariana Vieira da (2012) 'Políticas públicas de saúde: tendências recentes', *Sociologia, Problemas e Práticas* n° 69, 121–8.

Silva, Pedro Adão e (2002) 'O modelo de welfare da Europa do Sul: reflexões sobre a utilidade de um conceito', *Sociologia, Problemas e Práticas* n° 38, 25–59.

Silva, Pedro Adão e and Pereira, Mariana Trigo (2012) 'Entre os insiders e os midsiders: a proteção no desemprego em Portugal', *Sociologia, Problemas e Práticas* n° 70, pp. 133–150.

Sullivan, O. (2004) 'Changing gender practices within the household: A theoretical perspective', *Gender and Society* 18(2): 207–22.

Tobio, C. (2001) 'Working and mothering: Women's strategies in Spain', *European Societies* 3: 339–71.

Torres, A. (2008) 'Women, gender and work: The Portuguese case in the context of the European Union', *International Journal of Sociology* 38(4): 36–56, http://www.analiatorres.com/artigos.html

Torres, A., Mendes, R. and Lapa, T. (2008) 'Families in Europe', *Portuguese Journal of Social Science* 7(1): 49–84, http://www.analiatorres.com/artigos.html

Torres, Anália e Lapa, T. (2010) in 'Familia e jóvenes en Europa, Convergencia e diversidad' *Revista de Estúdio de Juventud*, Instituto de la Juventud, Espagna, pp. 11–32, http://analiatorres.com/artigos.html

Torres, Anália e Silva, F. V. (1999) 'Childcare and division of work between men and women', WORC Paper, 99.01.001/6, University of Tilburg, http://www.analiatorres.com/outraspublicacoes.html

Torres, Anália, Silva, F. V., Monteiro, T. L. and Cabrita, M. (2001) *Men and Women Between Family and Work*, Tilburg: Tilburg University Press, http://www.analiatorres.com/livros.html.

Torres, Anália (2010) Mudanças na Família: O privado na agenda pública, *Provas de Agregação, ISCTE-IUL*, http://analiatorres.com/provasagregacao.html.

Vasconcelos, P. (2005) 'Redes sociais de apoio', in Karin Wall (org.), *Famílias em Portugal. Percursos, Interações, Redes Sociais*, Lisboa: Imprensa de Ciências Sociais, pp. 599–631.

Wall, K. (Org.). (2005) *Famílias em Portugal Percursos, Interações, Redes Sociais*, Lisboa: ICS.

Wall, K. and Amâncio, L. (eds) (2007) *Família e Género em Portugal e na Europa*, Lisboa: Imprensa de Ciências Sociais.

Wall, K., Aboim, S. and Cunha, V. (2010a) *A Vida Familiar no Masculino: negociando velhas e novas masculinidades*, Lisboa: CITE.

Wall, K., Aboim, S. and Leitão, M. (2010b) *Observatório das Famílias e das Políticas de Família, Relatório*, Lisboa: Insituto de Ciências Sociais da Univeridade de Lisboa.

REDEFINING THE DYNAMICS OF INTERGENERATIONAL FAMILY SOLIDARITY IN SPAIN

Jordi Caïs and Laia Folguera

Department of Sociology and Organizational Analysis, Universitat de Barcelona, Barcelona, Spain

ABSTRACT: This article analyses the dynamics of family solidarity in Spain. The existing literature so far has defined the Spanish caring model as familistic due to the primacy of the family in the protection of dependants. However, this article shows that recent data on Spaniards' preferences concerning the care of their family dependents might question the sustainability of the bases of such model. This is consistent with the results of the OASIS Project, according to which societal changes may be leading to family care becoming less duty-driven and more dependent on personal affection and attachment.[1] The Spanish welfare state is labelled as familistic because family makes up for the lack of public benefits dampening adverse economic cycles and the problems of its more fragile members: children, young people and, especially, the elderly. Family solidarity is considered beneficial because it contains public spending and generates positive effects of solidarity and security in the population. Moreover, the expectations of the dependent elderly are focused on family, not on social services that always have been scarce in Spain and they are worsening with the economic crisis. But the Spanish welfare state based on familist values appears to be increasingly ineffective and more difficult to sustain. This article explains how changes in family structure and dynamics, along with the high rates of female labour force that Spain has recently achieved, affect family caregiving preferences and strategies.

1. The five-country (Norway, England, Germany, Spain and Israel) OASIS study collected data from representative, age-stratified, urban–community samples of about 1200 respondents in each country.

1. Introduction[2]

The Spanish welfare state is labelled as familistic due to the primacy of the family in the protection of dependants. In Spain, mechanisms of family solidarity ensure minimum levels of well-being where public policies do not provide coverage. Nowadays, in spite of governments' efforts to promote familist values in some centre and North-European countries, the Spanish welfare state based on familism may be in crisis. The social and economic context has changed and, while in Spain intergenerational solidarity within the family still enjoys social prestige, people can hardly spend so much time caring for their relatives as they did before. In the 'Parsonian' family model that characterizes familist societies, women are in charge of caring for dependent relatives. However, nowadays this model generates moral doubts. The 'second demographic transition' (Van de Kaa 1987) has arrived later in Spain than in northern and central Europe, albeit abruptly. Spanish population is ageing very quickly, with a significant impact on society. On the one hand, from 1990 to 2010 life expectancy in Spain has increased five years, reaching 82, and the percentage of population over 64 years old has increased by more than 3% to over 16% of the total Spanish population (INE 2012). On the other hand, Spanish women are no longer socialized to exercise the role of housewife. They have acquired the same level of education than Spanish men and they are joining the labour market in proportions similar to those of countries in central Europe. Moreover, at present, most Spanish families with children need two wages to get rid of the risk of falling into poverty. The welfare state in Spain has not developed social services to substitute for the role women have traditionally played through informal caring. As an example Spain has one of the lowest rates of kinder-garden services per capita as well as the one of the scarcest services in Europe for the caring of elderly dependence (Moreno and Bruquetas 2011), a situation that is worsening as a result of the current economic crisis. Spanish families react to the limited social policies of the Spanish welfare state by having fewer children, but it is not possible to 'have fewer grandparents'. For many families, combining professional activities with care for elderly dependents has become a problem that is difficult to solve.

This article analyses changes in the dynamics of family solidarity in Spain. We focus on how changes in family structure and dynamics, and the high rates of female labour force that Spain has recently achieved, affect family caregiving strategies. We also study whether people still care for reasons related to reciprocity, affection or duty, and to what extent the

2. We thank Marga Mari-Klose for her help and comments on the multivariate statistical analysis.

scarcity of public services and the high cost of private services are important as explanatory variables of the Spanish high rates of family caregivers.[3] Most of the studies on intergenerational family solidarity analyse whether a generous welfare state could undermine family solidarity. However, in the case of Spain, the question should be the opposite: can the Spanish model of elder care based on family solidarity remain unchanged taking into account the changes that have occurred in the family and the labour market? How sustainable is the Spanish model of elder care based on the generational contract between parents and adult children in the new socioeconomic context, where crisis has led to a substantial decrease in the public resources spent on social services for dependents?[4] And finally: Has intergenerational family solidarity weakened? Have new social realities, such as gender equality and increased female participation in paid work, influenced the ways in which filial norms are translated into emotional and instrumental support and help? Is family care becoming less duty-driven and more dependent on personal affection and attachment? All these questions are particularly relevant when we take into account recent data on Spaniards' preferences concerning dependence care, which might challenge the bases of intergenerational family solidarity, and which we analyse later on in this article.

2. Theoretical frame

It is widely accepted that interpersonal relationships among family members remain within the private sphere and that the process of receiving and providing care within families is mainly based on affection and reciprocity. Gouldner (1960) states that there is an implicit contract between generations within the family. Parents are required to invest a high proportion of their resources in the care of children. Therefore, when these parents get older, they expect that the provision of care will be reversed so that children should invest resources in caring for parents. Marshall *et al.* (1987) states that the nature of caring relationship is based on a delicate balance between reciprocity, affection and duty.

The welfare system based on the caring role of family networks enjoys considerable legitimacy among academics and politicians for being 'natural', 'altruistic' and because it develops quite effectively the functions

---

3. Coverage rates of social services for dependent elderly (home care services and nursing, among others) do not reach even 5% of people over 65 (Tobío *et al.* 2010).
4. In the recent electoral campaign that led to the victory of the new PP government, this political party openly acknowledged that some social programs for the dependents would have to be suspended until the economic situation improves.

entrusted to it (Marí- Klose and Marí-Klose 2006). They also argue that the model is very strong since it enjoys a wide social acceptance in southern Europe, where intergenerational family solidarity is understood as an unwavering value. The Spanish welfare regime is a clear example of the Mediterranean familistic welfare state model. Spanish public policies of social protection primarily ensure the safety of the family as an economic unit. But, in return, they expect the family to take care of most needs of its members. Family makes up for the lack of public benefits dampening adverse economic cycles and the problems of its more fragile members: children, young people and, especially, the elderly. Family solidarity is considered beneficial in every way: on the one hand, it contains public spending and, on the other hand, it generates positive effects of solidarity and security in the population. Therefore, the state is reluctant to provide social services in order not to discourage family informal care and breaking the intergenerational family contract.

In the past three decades, the family in Spain has been affected by a profound change that affects their ability to care for their dependent members, especially the elderly disabled. The inherited social rules that have defined the structure and roles of family members in the past have become obsolete. The figure for women exclusively devoted to housework and caring for children, parents and husband is dying (Marí-Klose and Marí-Klose 2006). Taking care of dependent people mainly by women is increasingly seen as unfair (Brullet and Torrabadella 2004). Often, Spanish families with children need two salaries to live without economic woes, and women have joined the labour market (Iglesias de Usel et al. 2009). For many families, combining professional activities with care for elderly dependent has become a problem, and in many cases the person taking care has been forced to abandon their work. In addition, the emergence of new family models such as single parents and blended families (Flaqué et al. 2006) generate new challenges for family solidarity.

The present article addresses two hypotheses. Our first hypothesis is that changes in family structure and dynamics, together with increasing participation of women in the labour market in Spain, are influencing people's preferences about how to care for dependants: care is becoming less duty-driven and more dependent on personal affection and attachment. Our second hypothesis is that dependants care is less understood as a moral duty that has to be assumed personally, and more as a responsibility that may be addressed through different means. We want to test whether a bad economic situation or a poor family network lead to a higher probability to prefer social care instead of family care. This hypothesis is in line with the theoretical frame of 'packaging and patchworking' describes (Knijn 2004). This theory states that families, especially women, combine all kinds of resources to carry out care for dependants. They do so regardless of the availability of social services offered by the state or even changes in that offer. This is a theoretical model that Knijn adapted from the concept of 'income packaging' introduced by Rainwater *et al.* (1986). They studied the combination of resources used by poor American families to overcome difficult periods of unemployment and illness. We want to test whether this hypothesis offers an explanation on how Spanish family caregivers would prefer to combine services trying to make care and work compatible.

3. The approach to the problem

In this section, we describe firstly the phenomenon of incorporation of Spanish women into the labour market in the last 15 years, which is higher to that of any other European country. Secondly, we emphasize that, despite these changes, the disabled people are still cared mostly by members of their own family. We highlight that the lack of public policies addressed to dependants in Spain is a possible explanation for the high number of Spaniards who have to take care by themselves for their dependent relatives. Finally, we show data about the consequences that taking care of a dependent relative has to the caregivers for their position in the labour market. Often, the difficulties of combining working life with taking care of dependent relatives force the caregiver to abandon his/her paid work. These three main points may help understand why the data presented in the next section – about the preferences for who should care for dependent relatives –, might question the basis on which the Spanish familistic model is founded.

The increasing individualization of society has profoundly altered the structure and functioning of the family (Beck 1986). Individual rights have been prefixed to the family institution (Meil 2006). Individualization implies less social control over individual life projects in the family. The variety in choices of way of lives is now broader, especially for women, who move from a life model oriented to family service to another in which they assert their right to have also an own career. In Spain, the number of women who are dedicated exclusively to home and who are the foundation on which familism rests has been halved in the last two decades. In 1988, 42% of women were engaged only in household chores. In 2008 this figure had fallen to 23%. At present, less than a quarter of Spanish women of working age are engaged in household chores. Furthermore, these women devoted exclusively to household chores are much older. In 1988 nearly 35% of housewives were older than 55 years old. Twenty years later, in 2008, this proportion had risen to almost 50% (Tobío *et al.* 2010). Moreover, in the last two decades a large number of Spanish women have

TABLE 1. Female activity rate in countries of UE15, 1999–2009

	Female activity rate		Female part-time employment (% total employment)	
	2009	Increase 1999–2009	2009	Increase 1999–2009
Spain	64.8%	14.8%	23.0%	5.9%
Greece	56.5	6.2	10.4	0.4
Italy	51.1	5.6	27.9	12.3
Portugal	69.0	6.1	16.4	− 0.3
Germany	71.4	8.4	45.3	7.9
Belgium	60.9	4.6	41.5	4.6
France	66.3	4.0	29.8	− 1.6
Denmark	77.3	1.2	37.9	3.2
Finland	73.5	2.4	19.0	2.1
Holland	74.1	8.9	75.8	6.9
Sweden	78.9	2.1	41.2	7.9
United Kingdom	69.5	1.6	42.5	− 1.5
UE15	65.9	6.6	37.0	3.8

Source: EUROSTAT, *Employment in Europe, 2010* (Luxembourg, European Commission: 2010).
Note: Female activity rates are calculated as the total amount of female laboure force (employed
and unemployed) as a share of total population in the corresponding age bracket.

entered into the labour market and female employment rates have been
growing rapidly. In 20 years, Spain has increased female participation
rate in 25%. It has gone from being the country with the lowest female
participation rate in the EU, to have a volume of female labour force
comparable to that of France, Germany or the UK. Table 1 compares the
female activity rates in different countries of the EU15 and shows that, in
the last decade, female participation rate in Spain has grown 15 percentage
points – much faster than in other countries. This rate has increased from
50% in 1999 to 65% in 2009 and almost reaches the female activity rate of
the EU15 average.[5]

Despite the changes in family and houshold structure and the
incorporation of women in the labor market, older people with disabilities

5. The Spanish female activity rate today is close to that of countries like France or
   Germany with conservative welfare regimes. And if we consider that the percentage of
   women working part time in Spain (23%) is much lower than that of women working
   part time in France (30%) and Germany (45%), we could think that the level of
   incorporation of Spanish women into the labor market is even higher than in those
   countries. The same thing happens in Britain with a model of liberal welfare state
   based primarily on the labor market. UK has a female activity rate of 70% which is
   five percentage points higher than Spain, but 42.5% of women working part time,
   while in Spain it's only 23%. Only Scandinavian countries with a welfare state model
   which makes special emphasis on sharing family responsibilities, have employment
   rates above the Spanish.

are still being cared primarily by family members – mostly women. A survey on disability, personal autonomy and dependency situations by National Institute of Statistics (INE) in 2008 shows that 55% of people who need care receive them from their families, mainly from children, and secondly from the spouses. Three out of four primary caregivers of dependent people in Spain are women. In fact, the profile of the usual caregiver in Spain is a woman (usually the daughter) between the ages of 45 and 64 of the same family, and residing in the same household as the person who is being taken care of. For many Spanish families to take care of their disabled members is the only option, as social assistance for families with disabled people is marginal in Spain, and often families cannot afford the high prices of private professional home-care or private residences for the elderly. The Spanish public network of services for dependence is fragmented and achieves low coverage rates in comparison with neighbouring countries.[6]

Sarasa (2007) makes a comprehensive contribution to understand factors that link social class and family solidarity. In Spain, on the one hand, poor health and risk of disability is higher among lower social classes, so the dependency ratio of the elderly is higher in low-income households. On the other hand, the use of care services is more frequent in households with higher disposable incomes and higher level of education. The level of disposable income is a good indicator to understand the use of private and public services: higher income implies higher capacity of access to private services and vice versa. Even though, Sarasa points out that the assumption that to have lower income implies more access to the scarce public social services is not clear, since there are other variables involved, such as educational level and cultural capital (the higher cultural capital the greater the ability to seize opportunities that public system offers).

The shortage of public policies for dependants in Spain may help understand the caring role of families in this country. Using data from OASIS project, Daatland and Lowenstein (2005) argue that intergenerational solidarity is substantial both in northern and southern welfare states, and seems to vary in character more than in strength. However, the difference in the volume of services and the access between public services offered by the Norwegian and the Spanish welfare state makes the experience to take care in Norway and in Spain hardly

---

6. The evidence of this weakness was acknowledged by the out coming socialist government, and used as the main argument for the approval of the 2006 dependency low. Despite the social and political expectations put on this low, its implementation was initially jeopardized by the scarce resources allocated to it, and afterwards by the economic crisis.

comparable.[7] Southern European states consider caring a private matter that has to be internalized within the family and Scandinavian states have assumed the societal responsibility of caring for their dependent citizens (Sarasa and Mestres 2007). On the one hand, The National Background Report for Norway's EUROFAMCARE (2004) indicates that in 2000 the Norwegian family caregivers spent on average just over two hours caring for their relatives. Norwegians prefer public services to the care of the family because they respond better to the needs of older people and their families. Older Norwegians expect emotional support rather than care from their families. On the other hand, the White Paper on Dependency in Spain (Ministerio de trabajo y Asuntos Sociales 2005) indicates that in 2004 Spanish family caregivers were involved in caring for their dependent relatives an average of ten hours a day. In Spain the family is the source of major support and care for the elderly; public services are scarce and families are not familiarized with them.[8] The expectations of the dependent elderly are focused on family, not on social services. Normally, children are those who have to take on the responsibility that taking care of them entails. Family support networks are very important to understand the use of public and private services that attend dependents in Spain. Single, divorced and separated people are those who most often have to resort to the market, volunteers or public social services (Sarasa 2007).

Being the main caregiver of a disabled person in Spain often is a full time job, incompatible with participation in the labour market. This affects the level of family income and, in some cases, the family risks to fall into poverty levels. One out of five caregivers state that he/she has economic problems (INE 2008). Sarasa and Billingsley (2008) argue that there exists a trade-off between caregiving to aged parents and paid employment, pulling children out of the labour market when parents' needs are great and no alternative resources are available. The demanding characteristics of taking care of someone in Spain, in many cases, makes caring incompatible with the possibility to work in the labour market – 25% of caregivers said that they found themselves in this situation – (INE

7. Bazo and Ancizu (2004) use in-depth interviews conducted in Norway, Germany, United Kingdom, Israel and Spain during the OASIS Project to explain the interactions service-person-family that occur in countries with different welfare state models and policies to support families. Their study finds that the possibility of access to social services determines different patterns of interaction and caring relationships between dependent parents and their children.
8. In villages, familiarity with social services is even lower than in cities. The scarcity of formal resources, both public and private, in municipalities under 50,000 inhabitants forces families to take care of their dependents even more than what families of large and medium cities have to assume (Sarasa 2007).

2008). In many cases the need to care for an elderly dependent forces the family to give up an additional salary. According to Sarasa (2008), Spain shares with other countries with Conservative and Mediterranean welfare regimes a similar bias in favour of cash transfers towards the elderly and handicapped.[9] And a policy focused on cash transfers is not neutral at all; in comparison with service provision, cash transfers reduce the opportunities of conciliation between paid work and care giving demands.

The Spanish model of elder care based on family solidarity involves very high economic and social costs for Spanish families. Spaniards are becoming more aware of it because, according to the Barometer of the Sociological Research Centre, two out of three Spaniards would be willing to pay more taxes to finance support services for families (CIS 2004). It is may be the case that such costs and the difficulties facing today Spanish families when caring for their dependants have affected Spaniards' preferences about the type of help they should offer to their dependents.

4. Spaniards' preferences concerning dependence care: Recent trends

In this section we analyse recent data on Spaniards' preferences concerning dependence care, which might challenge the bases of intergenerational family solidarity. We have created a logistic regression model using data from the CIS Barometer September 2010 (Table 2).[10] The dependent variable is a dummy variable constructed on the bases of a survey question where the respondent has to choose between social services and family care in the case of a dependent elder familiar. The reference category in the statistical model is: to agree that when a person cannot care for oneself it is better to rely on social services rather than on family. The independent variables include economic status and variables related to the structure, dynamics, and quality of family relationships, and confidence in the public social services. As statistical control variables the model includes age, sex, municipality size, educational level, religion and marital status.

We want to determine whether Spaniards' preferences concerning the care for their dependants increasingly resemble what the theoretical frame

---

9. Pensions and other transfers make up the bulk of expenditure, and, theoretically, beneficiaries can buy the services they need in the market but this possibility is realistically limited to a minority and thus reinforces inequalities (Sarasa and Mestres 2007).

10. The data for this multivariate analysis are from CIS Study 2844: Barometer of September 2010. A representative sample of 2473 Spanish people stratified by gender, age, autonomous regions and municipality size were interviewed in their homes about family values.

TABLE 2. Logistic regression model Dependent variable: to agree that when a person cannot care for oneself it is better to rely on social services rather than on family

	BLOCK1	BLOCK2	BLOCK3	BLOCK4	BLOCK5	BLOCK6
Sociodemographic variables						
Age[1]						
25 to 50	1	1	1	1	1	1
51 to 65	1,474**	1,548**	1,556**	1,550**	1,472**	1,408*
More than 65	1,491**	1,507**	1,540**	1,523**	1,357	1,296
Sex						
Male		1	1	1	1	1
Female		1,029	1,027	1,024	1,043	1,081
Size of the Town						
More than 1 million		1	1	1	1	1
From 100.001 to 100.000		0,701	0,721	0,712	0,717	0,697
From 10.001 to 100.000		0,642*	0,653*	0,647*	0,629*	0,632*
Since 10.000		0,739	0,760	0,754	0,734	0,709
Educational Level						
University		1	1	1	1	1
Secondary		1,352	1,226	1,232	1,139	1,190
Primary		1,104	1,047	1,048	1,018	1,060
Religiosity						
No believer		1	1	1	1	1
Believer		0,678**	0,675**	0,672**	0,659**	0,679**
Marital Status						
No married		1	1	1	1	1
Married		0,758*	0,791	0,790	0,794	0,873
Economic situation[2]			1,144	1,149	1,094	1,064
Degree of confidence on social services				1,011	1,012	1,028

TABLE 2 (Continued)

	BLOCK1	BLOCK2	BLOCK3	BLOCK4	BLOCK5	BLOCK6
Variables of structure and internal family dynamics						
Number of potential caregivers						
More than 6					1	1
From 3 to 5					1,156	1,091
From 0 to 2					2,348***	2,029**
Degree of family cohesion[3]						1,131**
Degree of satisfaction with the family						
High						1
Medium						1,376*
Low						3,182**
R2 Nagerkelke	1,1%	3,2%	3,5%	3,5%	7%	9%
Number of cases	1.494	1.494	1.494	1.494	1.494	1.494

. Level of signification 10%.

* Level of signification 5%.

** Level of signification 1%.

*** Level of signification 1/000.

Source: CIS N° 2844 Study Barometer September 2010 (Center for Sociological Research).

Notes: 1 The Matrix, having selected only those over 25, consists of 2234 cases.

2 The scale ranges from very good to very bad economic situation.

3 We constructed an index variable from two variables: 'visit or see their families, although there is no reason for it' and 'celebrates important dates (birthdays, Christmas, etc.) with members of his/her family. The family index ranges from more to less family cohesion.

of 'packaging and patchworking' describes. To this end, it will be useful to see whether the economic situation of the family affects its disposition to care their older relatives. It is also important to see whether the degree of confidence that families have in social services has any influence on their disposition to rely on them. We also want to find out whether people with weak family networks will tend to prefer a model where public social service provision is more present. Finally, we will see whether factors such as quality of relationships among family members affect the desire to provide care for elderly dependent relatives.

The results of the logistic regression analysis shows, in the first block, that age is a significant variable in its three categories without controlling for the other variables in the model. At first sight it would seem that intergenerational solidarity is even reinforced. The odds ratio of considering that an elderly dependant should go to social services rather than to rely on one's family is higher in the middle generation (51 to 65 years old) and in the older generation (more than 65 years old) than in the younger (25 to 50). With this data it seems that young people are even more willing to offer aid than elderly people. However, once we introduce the variables of structure and family relationships in the model, age is no longer significant for the group of people over 65 years old, and it only remains so for the group of 51 to 65. We conclude, therefore, that it is in the group that fits the higher frequency of caregiving where it is more common to find people who think that when a family dependant cannot care for oneself it is better to rely on social services rather than on family. This age group frequently has to confront the dilemma of having to juggle their work outside home and take care of the dependent family members.

In the second block of the logistic regression model we find the socio-demographic variables that are used for statistical control. The only ones that remain significant after introducing the variables of structure and family relationships are the size of the town where the respondent resides and religiosity. In small towns (10,000 to 100,000 inhabitants), the odds ratio of considering that it is better to rely on social services for the care of family dependants rather than on family care is about half in comparison to large cities with more than one million inhabitants. People's religiosity is also closely linked to family solidarity. The probability that a religious person expresses a preference for family caring of dependants instead of relying on social assistance doubles that among non-religious people.

In the third block of the model we introduce the economic situation of the interviewee, which is only slightly significant. At first sight, it would seem that, when a person is in a bad economic situation, the probability that he/she prefers that people who cannot care for themselves turn to public services rather than to family would increase. However, the model shows that, when we introduce the variable of family structure and relationships among its members, the economic variable loses its significance.

In the fourth block of the model we can observe that the degree of confidence in social services is not significant and explains nothing. This indicates that prioritizing social services rather than family care does not depend on having confidence in the quality of social services. As Bazo and Ancizu (2004) argue, Spaniards attach very little value to social services, know even less about them, and have little information about how they work.

The fifth and sixth blocks' variables are related to the structure and internal dynamics of the family. The results show that Spaniards' preferences for family dependants' caring options – social services or family care-, depend on such family features as human capital (number of potential caregivers), degree of family cohesion, and emotional wellbeing with family members. First, human capital, understood as the number of potential caregivers that a person think he can count on if necessary, is important. For someone with a limited number of people who could take care of him/her, the odds ratio of considering that it is better to rely on social services for the care of family dependants rather than on family care doubles that of someone with a great human capital. Second, the degree of family cohesion is also an important and significant variable. In families where there is frequent contact between its members, where they visit each other frequently and where they share feasts regularly, the likelihood that you prefer that social services primarily take care of elderly dependent family members is lower than in less cohesive families. Finally, the degree of satisfaction with the family exerts a determinant and statistically significant bearing on the probability of preferring social services in front of family care as a caring option for the family dependants. The probability of preferring social services is 30% higher if you have a medium satisfaction with your family and 220% higher if the degree of satisfaction with your family is low. Taking care of your parents when they need it is no longer an unavoidable obligation in Spain. Our data indicates that it depends on the quality of the relationship between parents and children.

This last finding is empirically relevant because it questions the sustainability of the Spanish model as it has been defined so far by the existing literature. Moreover, this finding is consistent with recent conclusions of the OASIS Project comparing five countries (Norway, Germany, United Kingdom, Israel and Spain). 'Family exchanges may be becoming less duty-driven and more open to individual variation, and personal affection and attachment may be increasingly important for family cohesion and inter-generational ties. Normative obligations live on, but may increasingly be modified by affection and choice, so that family relationships are transforming' (Lowenstein and Daatland 2006: 219).

Just as a way to illustrate this finding we use data from a few qualitative in-depth interviews from the COGEASDO study.[11] From the interviews to people older than 65 we note that the feeling of obligation to take care of their parents is very strong. Most people interviewed in this generation say that they take care of their parents at home because they loved them and they wanted to make sure they received the best care. But they also pointed out a sense of obligation to those who had taken care of them, educated, and emotionally and financially helped them throughout life. Nevertheless, some people interviewed from this generation do not share these feelings of affection and obligation to their parents due to problems of poor relationship between them or even because their parents were not caregivers. Even so they feel forced to take care of their parents due to the strength of social norms, as in the case of the following testimony:

> The relationship with my parents was cold because we stood apart during the days of childhood. [. . .] I was born during the war. During the post-war period my family had problems. My mother sent me to live with my grandmother. I lived with my grandparents until they died, and I knew my parents when I was grown up. [. . .] However, I took care of my mother. I could not take care of my father because he was self-sufficient until he died. [. . .] We always took care of my mother. I think that it was a kind of duty. If I had had a bad relationship with her, we would have taken care of her anyway.[12]

As shown in this excerpt, individual factors such as the case of inter-generational reciprocity were not a necessary condition to take care of parents. The explanation is due rather to the existence of strong normative social constructions. This is even clearer in the case of people who have to take care of people for whom they have no affection or debt (for example,

11. The Generational Contract Modification and Home Care Policy Project (COGEASDO) were founded under the National Plan of R + D of the Spanish Ministry of Science and Technology. Spaniards from two different generations were interviewed in order to see whether there have been changes in the generational contract within the family. The first generational group interviewed consists on people over 65 years. Women from this generation have been educated as homemakers and have cared for their parents. The second group interviewed consists on people from 30 to 50 years old. Unlike their parents, usually the two partners are active in the labor market. We want to find out whether they would be willing to care for their parents if necessary. Both groups were stratified by gender and social class (depending on household income and profession).

12. A 68 year-old man, who is an engineer and worked in textile companies and automotive, interviewed on 19 May 2006 at his home in Barcelona.

in-laws or widowed aunts and uncles) or even for people with whom you have a bad relationship. In these cases, what counts is the duty. A duty that is linked to social norms, as it is shown in this passage:

> We were poor but my husband's mother was from a rich family. She wanted his son to marry a girl with more money than me. She was widowed very young and because of that she leaned heavily on her son. She never accepted me. [...] We had an extremely bad relationship. She even hit me and wanted to kill me, but it was me who took care of her. I have never been able to forgive everything she did. I took care of her because it was my duty, because it was my mother-in-law, if it had not been the case, I hadn't done so. [...] My husband always supported me. Otherwise, I would have gone. It upset me that my children grew up in this environment and that they hated her. My life was very hard until she died.[13]

Some of the interviews made to people from the generation of 30 to 50 years old showed that the social norm of taking care of an elderly dependant under any circumstance is not as strong. Increasingly, the decision of taking care of elderly dependent family members personally depends on the quality of the relationship you have had with them. The arguments of this 39 years old woman with divorced parents provide a good example:

> I feel responsible for my mother, but not so much for my father. This is due to a poor relationship with him, nothing else. It's always been like this. If the relationship had been more or less good with both, I would have felt responsible for both. The problem is that it was bad with one of them.[14]

In other interviews, it is shown that it is difficult to break a social norm as strong as the obligation to take care personally of your parents. In many people interviewed we found a dichotomy between rhetoric and practice. Interviewees create an acceptance speech and even protection of the standard of being a caregiver. But for them the meaning of 'care' is not the same as for their parents and grandparents. When some interviewed people talk about the obligation of taking care of their parents, normally,

---

13. A 69 years old woman, who has worked all her life in a delicatessen, interviewed on 18 March 2006 at her home in Puigcerdá (Lerida).
14. A 39 years old woman married with two children. She studied psychology and is a college professor. Her parents are alive, in good health and self-sufficient. They got divorced many years ago. Interview on Saturday 25 March 2006 at 5 pm at her home in Terrassa (Barcelona).

they are not referring to take care of them by themselves. They mean that they will undertake to provide that care. This excerpt puts it clearly:

> We take care of them because it is our responsibility. I feel very responsible for my parents. We have always tried that they were well served. We have not done the work personally, like changing diapers, because we couldn't. If you have a job and children you cannot make such things. The solution is to put a person to look after them, and what we do is to control that person. We are always aware of how things go and if they are well served.[15]

As OASIS Project concluded, normative beliefs are sufficiently flexible to adapt to new social realities such as gender equality and increased female participation in paid-work (Lowenstein and Daatland 2006). There are different ways in which filial norms are translated into emotional and instrumental support and help. Having sufficient financial resources takes pressure off from the social norm, and therefore children are able to choose how far they will be involved eventually as caregivers of their parents. They can weigh up the pros and cons of their decision and, if they take care of their dependants, it will be more satisfying because it has been freely chosen. By contrast, most of the families that do not have sufficient financial resources to hire private care for their elderly dependants may feel they have no choice other than assuming such responsibility directly. As Sarasa and Billingsley (2008) concluded, in countries where home care is provided mainly by the market, as in Spain, is where we can find more social class inequalities. In fact, the poorer children cannot afford the services and they have to bear the care burdens more than the richest ones.

5. Conclusion

Caring for elder dependent parents is no longer perceived by the Spaniards as an unavoidable moral duty. Instead, the traditional preferences for family care over state care that have characterized the Spanish care model are strongly influenced by the existence of good personal relations among family members. Our analysis of recent data on Spaniards' preferences concerning the care of their family dependents shows that the degree of satisfaction with the family exerts a determinant and statistically significant bearing on the probability of preferring either

---

15. A 43 years old woman with three children. She is an entrepreneur, running a family business. She has people hired during the day. Somebody takes care of her mother and before somebody took care of her aunt. Interviewed on 11 July 2006 at her home in Sant Cugat del Vallès (Barcelona).

state or family care. The higher is the satisfaction with family relations, the higher is the probability of preferring family care; the lower such satisfaction, the higher the probability of preferring state care. Also, in families where there is not frequent contact between its members the likelihood of preferring social services is higher than in more cohesive families. Our findings could confirm our first hypothesis that new familiar realities, such as gender equity and increased female participation in paid work, make people's preferences about family care be less duty-driven and more dependent on personal affection and attachment.

Our findings partially confirm our second hypothesis. The data indicate that family network influence Spaniards' preferences concerning dependence care. People with poor family networks or little cohesive families have a higher probability of preferring to rely on state social services for the care of their dependants. The lower the number of potential caregivers, the more likely it is that they prefer social services. However, the economic situation does not have an influence on a preference for a particular way of caring for dependants. Our findings show that a bad economic situation does not necessarily lead to somebody preferring social assistance care for elderly dependants rather than family care.

Other interesting results of our study show that people in the age group between 51 and 65 show a higher probability to prefer state care for elder dependent relatives. This is the group that fits the higher frequency of caregiving and confronts more often the incompatibility between caregiving to aged parents and paid employment. Our data also indicate that preferences for social services over family care do not depend on either trust on or knowledge of such social services.

We can conclude that the profound economic and social changes in Spanish families may have changed the dynamics of family solidarity. Our study about preferences indicates that Spaniards no longer feel caring personally for their dependent parents as an unavoidable moral duty. Although it is difficult to break a social norm as strong as the obligation to take care personally of one's parents, normative beliefs are sufficiently flexible to adapt to new social realities such as gender equality and increased female participation in paid-work. In Spain, the generation contract by which children should care for their dependent parents is still alive, but nowadays such obligation is defined and understood in a more flexible way – that is, there are different ways in which filial norms are translated into emotional and instrumental support and help. In-depth interviews excerpts included in this article give us some clues for further interesting hypothesis for further research – for example, these interviews point out that, at least in some cases, sufficient financial resources may take pressure off the social norm of caring personally for them. However, a large majority of Spanish families do not have enough money to afford private services and have difficulties assuming the caring role given to family by the Spanish welfare state. This is even more relevant in a country where public resources devoted to elder care are extremely scarce.

Finally, some limitations of the data should be considered. First, the data we use in our statistical model are exclusively cross-sectional. A longitudinal design would have provided a more dynamic picture, but the necessary data to do so are not available. Second, the data we use give information about Spaniards' preferences in relation to who should take care of elder dependents – either family or the state. This is why we do not take for granted that preferences and dispositions are predicting future behaviours and practices. However, such data do allow us to analyse the strength of expressed filial obligations (normative solidarity). Third, the interview excerpts used in this article do not have analytical purposes, but are only aimed at illustrating the Spanish reality and better contextualize the statistical findings.

Acknowledgments

This article was drafted within the SOLFCARE project ("Solidaridad familiar, cambio actitudinal y reforma del Estado de bienestar en España: el familismo en transición"), under the Plan Nacional de I+D+i of the Spanish Government (CSO2011-27494).

References

Bazo, M. T. and Ancizu I. (2004) 'El papel de la familia y los servicios en el mantenimiento de la autonomía de las personas mayores: una perspectiva internacional comparada', *Revista Española de Investigaciones Sociológicas* 105: 45–73.
Beck, U. (1997 [1986]) *La sociedad del riesgo*, Barcelona: Paidós.
Brullet, C. and Torrabadella, L. (2004) 'La infància en las dinámicas de transformación familiar', in C. Gómez-Granell, M.G. Milá, A.R. Millet and C.P. Iglesias (eds), *Infancia y familias: realidades y tendencias*, Barcelona: Ariel, pp. 37–61.
CIS (2010) *Estudio CIS n° 2.844: Barómetro de se septiembre de 2010*, Madrid: CIS.
CIS (2004) *Estudio CIS n° 2.581: Barómetro de noviembre de 2004*, Madrid: CIS.
Daatland, S. O. and Lowenstein, A. (2005) 'Intergenerational solidarity and the family-welfare state balance', *European Journal of Ageing* 2: 174–82.

EUROSTAT (2010) *Employment in Europe, 2010*, Luxembourg: European Commission.

Flaqué, L., Almeda, E. and Navarro, L. (2006) *Monoparentalitat i infància*, Barcelona: Fundació la Caixa.

Gouldner, A. W. (1960) 'The norm of reciprocity', *American Sociological Review* 25: 161–78.

INE (2012) *Indicadores Demográficos básicos. Indicadores de crecimiento y estructura de la población. Series 1975–2010*, Madrid: INE

INE (2008) *Encuesta de discapacidad, autonomía personal y situaciones de dependencia: EDAD*, Madrid: INE.

Ingebretsen, R. and Eriksen, J. (2004) *EUROFAMCARE. Services for Supporting Family Carers of Elderly People in Europe: Characteristics, Coverage and Usage – National Background Report for Norway*, Oslo: NOVA. Norwegian Social Research.

Iglesias de Usel, J., Marí-Klose, P., Marí-Klose M. and González Blasco, P. (2009) *Matrimonios y parejas jóvenes. España 2009*, Madrid: Fundación SM.

Knijn,T. (2004) 'Family solidarity and social solidarity: substitutes or complements?', in T. Knijn and A. Komter (eds), *Solidarity between the Sexes and the Generations*, Cheltenham/Northampton: Edward Elgar, pp. 18–33.

Lowenstein, A. and Daatland, S. O. (2006) 'Filial norms and family support in a comparative cross-national context: Evidence from the OASIS study', *Ageing & Society* 26: 203–23.

Marí-Klose, P. and Marí-Klose, M. (2006) *Edad del Cambio: Jóvenes en los circuitos de solidaridad intergeneracional*, Madrid: CIS.

Marshall, V. W., Rosenthal, C. J. and Daciuk, J. (1987) 'Older parents' expectations for filial support', *Social Justice Research* 1(4): 405–24.

Meil, G. (2006) *Pares i fills a l'España actual*, Barcelona: Fundació la Caixa.

Ministerio de trabajo y Asuntos Sociales (2005) *El Libro Blanco de la Dependencia*, Madrid: Ministerio de trabajo y Asuntos Sociales.

Moreno, F. J. and Bruquetas, M. (2011) *Inmigración y Estado de bienestar en España*, Barcelona: Fundació la Caixa.

Tobio, C., Agulló, M. S., Gómez, M. V. and Martín-Palomo, M. T. (2010) *El cuidado de las personas: Un reto para el siglo XXI*, Barcelona: Fundació la Caixa.

Rainwater, L., Rein, M. and Schwarz, J. (1986) *Income Packaging in the Welfare State: A Comparative Study of Family Income*, Oxford: Oxford University Press.

Sarasa S. (2008) 'Do welfare benefits affect women's choices of adult care giving?', *European Sociological Review* 24(1): 37–51.

Sarasa, S. and Billingsley, S. (2008) 'Personal and household care giving from adult children to parents and social stratification', in C. Saraceno (ed.), *Families, Aging and Social Policy*, Cheltenham: Edward & Elgar, pp. 123–46.

Sarasa, S. (2007) 'La atención a las personas adultas dependientes en España: desigualdades territoriales y estratificación social', en V. Navarro (ed.), *La situación social de España II*, Madrid: Biblioteca Nueva, pp. 445–70.

Sarasa, S. and Mestres, J. (2007) 'Women's employment and the adult care burden', in G. Esping-Andersen (ed.), *Family Formation and Family Dilemmas in Contemporary Europe*, Bilbao: FBBVA, pp. 185–221.

Van de Kaa, D. J. (1987) 'Europe's second demographic transition', *Population Bulletin* 41: 1–57.

THE SOUTHERN EUROPEAN MIGRANT-BASED CARE MODEL

Long-term care and employment trajectories in Italy and Spain

Barbara Da Roit
Department of Sociology and Anthropology, University of Amsterdam
Amparo González Ferrer
Instituto de Economía, Geografía y Demografía (CSIC) Madrid
Francisco Javier Moreno-Fuentes
Instituto de Políticas y Bienes Públicos (CSIC) Madrid

ABSTRACT: The development of personal social services and female employment is intertwined, not only in the domain of childcare. With the ageing of the population, the changing forms of care and the developments in the eldercare labour market become crucial issues. The new risk of dependency represents a challenge, but also an opportunity. This paper provides an overview of the relationship between the development of long-term care policies and services in distinct European countries and female employment in the care sector. Whereas Northern European countries have developed policies in the field at an earlier stage and continental countries intervened with new policies in the last 10–15 years, in Southern Europe policies remain weak and fragmented. The paper concentrates on the case of Southern European countries, where the weakness of social policies and low development of services did not prevent the rise of a new care labour market. Next to still low employment rates among women, long-term care tends to be provided mainly by migrant care workers often in the underground economy regardless of their legal status. The last development is a key issue for Southern European countries, as discussed in the paper, not only for the current consequences on migrant workers, older people and their families, but also because it is likely to structure any possible future development in long-term care policies.

1. Introduction

The[1] literature devoted to analysing the relationship between women's labour market participation and welfare polices has generally focused on the effects of childcare services on female employment. Public and publicly regulated services for small children enable women to participate in the labour market, while simultaneously offering them employment opportunities. With the ageing of European populations employment linked to elderly care is becoming a crucial dimension as well: the 'new social risk' of dependency constitutes a challenge, but also an opportunity for European welfare systems (Taylor-Gooby 2004).

European policy makers view increasing female employment as key for the sustainability of welfare states, as well as for combating poverty and social exclusion (European Commission 2010). Simultaneously, the rising long-term care (LTC) needs of an ageing population put pressure on the funding and organisation of care schemes, as well as on the informal care provided by relatives (Pfau-Effinger and Rostgaard 2011). While the collective provision of care services represents an opportunity for female employment, it also constitutes a financial challenge, particularly in times of fiscal austerity.

This paper looks at the relationship between LTC policies and female employment in Southern European countries. The increasing care needs, alongside particularly rapid population ageing and decreasing fertility rates have put considerable strain on families in recent years. In absence of effective policy reforms that substantially reduce the responsibility of families in care provision, employment rates in the care sector remained relatively low. However, a private care market based mainly on informal immigrant labour has emerged. These developments have important consequences for Southern European societies, not only for the life and working trajectories of migrant workers, elderly people and their families, but also because of their implications for future development in LTC policies in these countries.

2. European Welfare regimes, LTC and female employment

The relationship between the social policies and the labour market structure represents a core issue within welfare regime theory (Esping-

1. This article was drafted within the SOLFCARE project ('*Solidaridad familiar, cambio actitudinal y reforma del Estado de bienestar en España: el familismo en transición*'), under the 'Plan Nacional de I + D + i, Spain' (programme code CSO2011-27494), and the research project 'Social policies for the elderly and children: preference formation and welfare reform', funded by Fundación CSIC-Caixa.

Andersen 1990). Each welfare regime has found a different solution to the classical cost-disease problem (Esping-Andersen 1999). By establishing a specific division of responsibilities between the private and the public/collective spheres, LTC policies contribute to amount and the type of employment relations in this sector. Next to affecting the number of available jobs, LTC policies foster employment within different types of organisations. The literature traditionally emphasised the importance of the public-private divide as the crucial variable explaining job quality and women's empowerment as service workers (Kolberg 1991). Moreover there is evidence of significant differences in the quality of work between non-profit and for-profit organisations (Rosenau and Linder 2003; McGregor *et al.* 2005; Meagher and Cortis 2009). In addition, policies might support the growth of employment within organisations or private employment relationships between individual care workers and care receivers.

In the present section, we review the evolution of LTC systems in distinct European welfare regimes and the differential impact on female employment.

2.1. LTC systems' transformation

In the early 1990s LTC arrangements in European countries clustered around four models. Cross-country diversity concerned the availability of publicly funded and regulated care services, legal obligations to care attributed to individuals and the degree and type of involvement of informal caregivers. While these differentiations reflects the classical typology of Welfare regimes, the recent socio-demographic transformations have created considerable tensions to the informal care giving arrangements, as well as to public LTC schemes paving the way, since the 1990s, to many changes in the domain of LTC policies, public management, and families' strategies.

In the Nordic countries and the Netherlands, LTC residential and home care services were traditionally more developed, reflecting a comparatively large public and/or a highly regulated non-profit sector (Anttonen and Sipila 1996). The social-democratic answer to LTC demands traditionally consisted in high public investments in care services, which fostered extensive and universally available service supply, together with the growth of personal services employment. However, it is notably in these countries that cost containment has been a dominant policy goal since the 1990s. This entailed stricter eligibility criteria for care beneficiaries, higher co-payments, contracting out of service provision to the private sector (for profit or not for profit) and quasi-market or market mechanisms in service provision, decentralisation and targeting schemes at the local level (Trydegard 2003; Szebehely and Trydegard 2012; Da Roit 2012). Increasing emphasis has been put on informal care often accompanied by cash transfers and consumer-choice models (Da Roit and Le Bihan 2010). These developments have questioned the inclusiveness and universalism of these systems (Trydegard 2003; Szebehely and Trydegard 2012; Da Roit 2012), while possibly containing the growth of and changing female employment in the care sector.

In the early 1990s in the UK LTC services were less developed than in the Scandinavian countries but more than in continental and southern Europe (Anttonen and Sipila 1996). However, the LTC sector was affected by the early privatisation trends in the 1980s, anticipating similar developments in Northern European countries. As such, the liberal welfare regime solution to LTC challenges consists in the limited public intervention and regulation of the care sector, allowing wide accessibility to private services (through the creation of low-waged and low-protected jobs) that would be otherwise inaccessible to large section of the population. In recent years these features have been accentuated through an explicit marketisation strategy of care services with important consequences on employment in the sector.

Continental European countries and even more so Southern European countries have always been little involved in formal care provision, expecting families to care for their members (Anttonen and Sipila 1996). The conservative-corporatist answer to LTC challenges, which found an extreme manifestation in Southern Europe, traditionally placed the burden of the production of services on (women within) families through self-production and unpaid care work (Esping-Andersen 1999; Folbre and Nelson 2000; Saraceno 2003). Here weak, fragmented and residual social policies went hand in hand withlegal obligations on family members (Millar and Warman 1996; Saraceno and Naldini 2007), and particularly intensive informal caregiving (Haberkern and Szydlik 2010). In the last two decades many continental European countries started to pay more attention to the LTC needs. New schemes aimed at providing a broader coverage to the risk of dependency were introduced in countries like Germany, Austria and France. In a time of welfare retrenchment, new social risks were recognised by the political system and translated into specific policies. Even if these new schemes predominantly rely on cash benefits (Da Roit and Le Bihan 2010) they contributed to increasing the supply of formal services (Da Roit and Sabatinelli 2012). By contrast, in Southern European little policy developments took place or were effective in increasing the availability of care services. The development of LTC services (public and/or private) remained marginal, implying weak employment potential in the formal service sector.

2.2. LTC development and female employment

Employment rates in 'Health and social work' of women aged 25 to 64 were well above 20% in Denmark and Sweden in the mid 1990s reflecting the characteristics of the social democratic welfare model. This proportion remained stable in Denmark while it decreased in Sweden in a 10-year period. The rates in all other countries were lower but increased everywhere over time. As a result, the original differences between the Nordic cluster and the UK on the one side and the continental European (France and Germany) countries on the other are sill there even if slightly reduced. Southern European countries considered do display a small growth, but given the starting point, they still lag behind (Table 1).

Despite important transformations, the distribution between employment in the public, profit and non-profit sector, continues to reflect the features of the original welfare models. In Sweden, where the process of marketisation has been the largest among the Nordic countries the bulk (ca 80%) of care work still takes place within public organisations. By contrast, in England profit providers currently cover three fourths of eldercare work (Brennan *et al.* 2012). Also in Germany and France, Italy and Spain non-profit organisations remain predominant notwithstanding the growing importance of for profit providers.

3. The Southern European trajectory: LTC and female employment in Italy and Spain

LTC policies in Southern Europe traditionally shared its basic traits with those of the continental corporatist welfare model as illustrated above. However, compared to most continental European countries, the debate on LTC emerged much later in this region, and when the issue was finally introduced in the political agenda, in the mid 2000s, it did not result in

TABLE 1. Employment rate of women aged 25–64 in 'health and social work' in selected EU countries

	1995	2005
Denmark	23.2	24.7
Sweden	29.3	22.8
UK	13.2	15.4
Germany	8.6	12.0
France	10.3	13.9
Italy	3.9	6.0
Spain	4.0	6.4

Source: Eurostat.

any substantial policy change (as it occurred in the case of Italy), or it produced only incomplete reforms (like in Spain) (Da Roit and Sabatinelli 2012).

At the same time important transformations in the care arrangements of older people in Southern Europe did occur despite any relevant or effective policy transformation or, most likely, partly as a result of a lack of effective policy initiative. Since the late 1990s a large care market developed in countries like Italy and Spain which official statistics can hardly capture due to its very nature. In Italy, for instance, it was estimated that between 0.7 and 1 million migrant care workers were working in 2005 (Mesini *et al.* 2006; Simonazzi 2009), which clearly outnumbered the workers in the formal care sector (Da Roit and Sabatinelli 2005). These workers are being directly employed by older people or their family members as domestic care workers, often without regular working contracts or permits to stay.

In what follows we first discuss the policy process in the two countries, then look at the significance of the newly emerged care market and at its implications for possible future developments.

3.1. Italy: the unintended centrality of cash-for-care and missed reforms

LTC in Italy features distinct policy fields based on heterogeneous and independent logics, eligibility criteria, organisation and funding.

The only national program is the '*indennità di accompagnamento*' (IdA - attendance allowance), a universalistic cash transfer for those certified as totally dependent, i.e. totally disabled, unable to perform everyday tasks, and requiring continuous care, independently of age. The IdA was introduced by the national government in the early 1980s as a scheme for adult disabled people, and it was extended to older dependant people a few years later as a consequence of a constitutional court decision. Unintendedly this program became the most important public intervention in favour of older dependant people in Italy, reaching today around 10–11% of people aged 65 + (more than 45% of the beneficiaries are older than 80) and absorbing the bulk of all resources employed for care policies (Da Roit 2006). This allowance ensures a flat-rate non–mean tested income supplement (498 € per month in 2013), and it does not involve any form of control on the use of the benefit.

In addition, local welfare schemes include the provision of residential and domiciliary services characterised by a complex division of responsibilities between public administrations, namely between health and social services agencies. The fragmentation of responsibilities, and the diversity of eligibility criteria are their most salient characteristic. While health services (medical and nursing services often provided in presence of acute care needs) are assigned on a universalistic basis and almost free of charge, social services (home care, nursing homes, assistance while staying in residential facilities) are provided by municipalities on the basis of highly selective and extremely varied criteria of access, largely determined by available budgets and the policy options adopted by individual local authorities.

The issue of LTC emerged in the Italian public and political agenda in the second half of the 1990s, when the national government appointed a commission of experts to provide an evaluation of the 'macro economic compatibility of social expenses' in the country.[2] The Onofri Commission pointed out, among other lines of reform, the need for a new scheme of protection in favour of elder dependent people. Nevertheless, such a policy advice was never translated into a reform of national LTC policies in Italy.

At the regional and local level there was a trend toward the introduction of a range of heterogeneous cash-for-care measures, enacted only by certain regions and municipalities, usually provided on the basis of a means-tested and selective criteria (mainly in case of severely disabled elderly). Despite the great geographical variation, these local welfare programmes cater for a small number of people, mostly in very advanced stages of dependency, and provide very weak services, generally with co-payments from the beneficiaries. The cash-for-care programs, and the services enacted by Italian regional and local authorities since the 1990s, have been of too little intensity as to produce any significant changes in the situation of dependent people and their families (Da Roit 2010). Despite clear evidence of the tensions due to the emerging care needs, Italian LTC policies have shown considerable inertia and lack of substantial development (Pavolini and Ranci 2008; Naldini and Saraceno 2008).

The reasons for the Italian policy stall in LTC are multifaceted. It has been argued that these should be found in the familistic approach to social policy (Pfau-Effinger 2005), and in the ideological divisiveness of the political system (Naldini and Saraceno 2008), next to the particularly tight budget constraints which hindered the political consensus on reforms (Boeri and Perotti 2002; Bonoli 2007). It has also been underlined that the form of the State, and the clientelistic and particularistic features of the Italian polity, did not support reform (Da Roit and Sabatinelli 2012). In this context the IdA continues to represent the main component of the

---

2. This commission was in charge of providing a general diagnosis of social expenditure, and of the coverage of social protection in a broad sense (including pensions, the health system and social benefits and services).

Italian LTC policy, and it has played a central role, both in the missed reform of the LTC system, and in the rise of the migrant care market. This scheme absorbs a large share of the resources available for social protection as a whole. Its beneficiaries represent a significant proportion of the disabled and the elderly, and the organisations of disabled people are actively involved in the administration of the scheme and in defending it against any substantial reform (Ranci *et al.* 2008). As a consequence, reforming LTC in Italy has become inherently equivalent to reforming the IdA, and this has represented an additional and important obstacle in the process of elaborating a more comprehensive policy response to this emerging social risk (Da Roit and Sabatinelli 2012).

Under the pressure of increasing care needs the IdA has contributed to the emergence of an informal care market. Working mainly as an income supplement with unconditional use, the IdA has favoured the recourse to the underground care market. This is consistent with the findings of a comparative analysis of the presence of migrant care workers employed by families, and according to which two conditions appear to be relevant next to the weak development of LTC services: the provision of uncontrolled cash benefits (like the IdA), and weak regulation of labour markets and migration flows (Da Roit and Weicht 2013). In Italy both conditions are simultaneously present.

3.2. Spain: Unfulfilled reform

In the case of the Spain a similar dichotomy between national programs in an embryonic stage of development, and a weak and patchy involvement of local and regional administrations defines public intervention in the domain of LTC. In contrast with the Italian case though, the need to develop LTC policies was clearly introduced in the Spanish political agenda in the early 2000s, and this produced comprehensive reform aimed at articulating a new LTC policy.

After a long and thorough policy debate, legislation was thus passed in 2006 (*Ley de Promoción de la Autonomía Personal y Atención a las Personas Dependientes*) with the explicit objective of providing universal access to LTC services on a need basis. This Law recognised the individual right to receive care for dependent people of all ages, based on a scale of dependency (moderate, severe and large, each one divided in two degrees of intensity) that was also used to establish the schedule for the deployment of the system.

While the right to receive care is recognised for every citizen, the funding is expected to come from a combination of public and private sources through the application of income-related co-payments. Public administrations are supposed to guarantee the access of every individual to the benefits, but the intensity of the public involvement depends on the income level of the beneficiary (Arriba González de Durana and Moreno Fuentes 2009).

The law aimed at promoting the provision of care services by public administrations (either directly, or in the cooperation with third sector organisations), alongside complementary and intendedly exceptional cash transfers, namely service vouchers, allowances for hiring personal assistance and compensating informal caregivers, The underlying policy objective was the emergence of a niche for jobs in the caring sector (Sarasa 2011).

This national LTC legislation came to complement the schemes already set up by regional and local administrations, which, similarly to the Italian case, had traditionally being strongly segmented and underfunded. The responsibility for the concrete definition of eligibility criteria was given to the regional and local authorities implementing those programs. The governance of the new programs and schemes was supposed to be based on the cooperation of the three levels of administration of the Spanish State: the national government, the autonomous regions and the municipalities. The financing of the costs f those programs was planned to be shared in equal thirds by the three levels of government (Costa-Font and Garcia Gonzalez 2007).

The way in which the implementation of this legislation will end up unfolding, and the specific impact it will have in the different Spanish regions, remains difficult to foresee a few years after the passing of that Law (Meil 2011; Sarasa 2011). The type of services or cash transfers to be provided to the final users, as well as the exact articulation of responsibilities (financial, regulatory, etc.) among the different public administrations, remain to be fully defined. The steps taken towards the implementation of this legislation, initially planned to be fully completed in 2015, seem to indicate a substantial delay, as well as a clear trend towards the establishment of systems of cash transfers instead of the provision of services which were supposed to characterise the new policy. The reason for the delays is to a large extent linked to the difficult situation of public finances in Spain since 2008. Between 2009 and 2012 the national government has been reducing its funding from around 40% (regions were covering some 50% and the remaining 10% came from users), to a little over 20% (regions were covering well over 60%, and beneficiaries were covering nearly 17% of the costs of the programs) (Barriga Martín et al. 2013). All levels of administration are lagging behind in the process of evaluating the applications of people in need of care, as well as in the recognition of the right to access the care schemes and programs. As a consequence, the total number of beneficiaries has been decreasing due to the fact that the mortality rate of the users is higher than the new take up rate. While the system reached its peak with some 780,000 beneficiaries in July 2012, from then on the number of beneficiaries decreased, and in December 2012 some 770,000 dependant persons were receiving some kind of benefit (Barriga Martín *et al.* 2013).

Moreover, while LTC legislation explicitly states that the priority of must be on the provision of services instead of on cash transfers, a bit more than 50% of the beneficiaries receives cash allowances, and only a bit more than 30% were receiving in-kind services. The preference of regional authorities for the cash allowances reflects the priority attributed to the cost-containment logic over the development of care services of a minimum quality and professionalisation. Cash transfers have not only lower costs, but also allow for a much more 'hands-off' approach by the regional authorities. The traditional weakness of the social services at the local and regional level, the lack of political will to fully implement these programs (most notably among conservative elected representatives), as well as the complexity of the multi-level governance of these programs also contribute to the option for the cheaper and less intensive forms of intervention (Sarasa 2011). This situation prevents the development of a niche for caring jobs that supports families by helping them care for dependent people, while greatly contributing to the emergence of an informal and precarious care market generally occupied by immigrant women.

3.3. Women's employment in the LTC sector in Italy and Spain

Important changes have taken place in LTC arrangements through the relatively unexpected growth of a private caring market in both countries based on domestic work and female immigration. These forms of employment are not very visible in official statistics.

LTC activities are often included under different occupational categories, depending on the formal qualifications of the employee, the age of the dependent person, the place where caring activities take place, etc. Moreover, many of these activities are often provided in the framework of 'domestic service' relations, which makes even more difficult to quantify them. In countries like Italy and Spain this situation is further complicated by the importance of grey labour in the domestic sector, the increasing use of immigrant labour to care for the elderly living at home since the late 1990s, and the combination of the two phenomena. Immigration in the Mediterranean countries is not only a relatively recent phenomenon, but one that has developed very rapidly. Two distinctive features of recent immigration patterns to both countries are, first, the large numbers of undocumented migrants, which represented a very significant share of the total stock of resident immigrants in both countries in some periods (Reyneri 2003; Cebolla and González-Ferrer 2008, 2013); and secondly, the concentration of immigrant workers in paid household work (Reyneri 2001; Colombo 2003). In fact, the large demand for caring work encouraged large inflows and stocks of irregular migrants, often facilitated by immigration policies based more on ex-post regularisations than on ex-ante planning of flows (Naldini and Saraceno 2008). To estimate the actual number of migrant carers in these two countries is even more difficult than for non-migrant workers due to the fact that an unknown proportion of migrants employed in care activities does not appear in official statistics.

Table 2 reports the number of national and foreign domestic workers registered in the Social Security System of Spain and Italy. The official domestic employment sector has enormously grown in the past two countries over time, largely due to the steadily increasing number of migrant workers. In 2000, the number of regularly registered foreign domestic workers was ca. 137,000 in Italy, and 48,000 in Spain vs. 120,000 and 105,000 nationals, respectively. In both countries the registered foreign population in the domestic sector has grown by 418% in Italy and 370% in Spain between 2000 and 2011/2012, compared to a much more modest increase by 45% among Italians and 82% among Spaniards in the same period. In 2011/2012 regular jobs in the domestic sector amounted to slightly less than 900,000 in Italy and slightly above 400,000 in Spain. In one decade 700,000 and over 300,000 new regular jobs have been created in this sector respectively. The proportion of migrants taking up these jobs at the end of the period is as high as 80% in Italy and 54% in Spain.

Changes in the size of the registered foreign population employed in the domestic sector clearly reflect changes in the rules affecting both registration and legal residence and work for immigrants, and particularly the implementation of amnesties for foreign (domestic) workers.

Significantly, the number of registered domestic workers in Italy was more than three times as high in 2002 compared to 2001 (from 140 to 419 thousand) and the proportion of migrants went from 52 to 76% in one year only at the time of the first regularisation procedure explicitly directed at migrant care workers. Similarly, the number went from 530 to 800 thousand between 2008 and 2009 at the time of a second amnesty. Something similar occurred in Spain in the regularisations of 2001 and, above all, in that of 2005. After these huge regularisation programs, care workers have been granted a special quota in the programmed yearly immigration flows in Italy, whereas in Spain a permanent mechanism for regularisation known as '*arraigo*' is available for those who can prove stable

TABLE 2. Registered domestic workers and foreign domestic workers in Italy and Spain, several years

	Italy					Spain				
	Registered Domestic Workers (thousands)		% Foreigners over Total	Annual growth in no. of registered workers		Registered Domestic Workers (thousands)		% Foreigners over Total	Annual growth in no. of registered workers	
	nationals	foreigners		nationals	foreigners	nationals	foreigners		nationals	foreigners
1991	145.4	35.7	19.7			n.a.	n.a.	n.a.	n.a.	n.a.
1995	125.2	67.7	35.1	-3.5	22.4	n.a.	n.a.	n.a.	n.a.	n.a.
2000 (b)	120.2	136.6	53.2	-0.8	20.4	104.9	48.0	31.4		
2001 (b)	130.1	139.9	51.8	8.2	2.4	103.7	54.5	34.5	-1.2	13.4
2002 (a)	134.2	418.9	75.7	3.2	199.4	103.9	84.2	44.8	0.3	54.6
2003	133.6	403.6	75.1	-0.4	-3.7	105.9	73.4	40.9	1.9	-12.8
2004	133.8	365.8	73.2	0.1	-9.4	107.7	76.4	41.5	1.7	4.1
2005 (b)	134.2	344.7	72.0	0.3	-5.8	110.9	253.8	69.6	3.0	231.9
2006	134.8	344.4	71.9	0.4	-0.1	113.4	186.7	62.2	2.1	-26.4
2007	139.7	484.4	77.6	3.6	40.7	116.3	152.8	56.8	2.6	-18.2
2008	147.6	531.6	78.3	5.7	9.7	115.7	170.3	59.6	-0.6	11.5
2009 (a)	164.3	799.0	82.9	11.3	50.3	113.8	175.3	60.6	-1.7	2.9
2010	168.6	746.9	81.6	2.6	-6.5	113.2	178.4	61.2	-0.5	1.8
2011	173.8	707.8	80.3	3.1	-5.2	113.5	181.4	61.5	0.2	1.7
2012(c)	n.a.	n.a.	n.a.	n.a.	n.a.	190.5	225.6	54.2	67.8	24.4
Growth 2000–11 (IT)	45	418	51							
2000–12 (ES)						82	370	73		

Sources: Italy: Inps, Osservatorio sul lavoro domestico (http://www.inps.it/webidentity/banchedatistatistiche/domestici/index.jsp); Spain: Ministry of Employment and Social Security (http://www.empleo.gob.es/series/).

(a) Amnesty for migrant (domestic) workers in Italy.

(b) Amnesty for migrant (domestic) workers in Spain.

(c) Change in domestic employment registration requirements in Spain.

attachment to the labour market, including the domestic sector. However, given the structural informality of this sector, as well as the short-term temporary solution provided by amnesties, the number of registered domestic migrant workers fell immediately after in both countries, and only recovered as a result of the new regularisation procedure implemented in 2008/2009 in Italy, and in Spain as a result of the reform of the system that regulate compulsory registration of domestic workers in 2012. Up to 2011, registration of domestic workers in Spain was mandatory only if the person worked more than 72 hours per month for a specific employer. However, as of 1 January 2012, people who employed domestic workers must register their employees in the social security system and pay contributions for them regardless of their monthly work hours. As can be seen in the last column of Table 2, registration of national domestic workers increased by 68% in comparison to the previous year, among the foreigners it increased only by 24%, which is pointing to the weaker position of foreign domestic workers in Spain.[3]

These figures on registered labour already show that under–registration is an issue, particularly but not only among foreigners. Labour force Survey (LFS) data confirm this view. Table 3 is based on the EU–LFS Survey and provides estimates of the number of women employed in different forms of care work in both countries, distinguishing between EU15 and non-EU15 workers.[4] In 2008, EU15 workers (which include mainly Spaniards) employed in the domestic sector were approximately 800,000 according to the EU–LFS, whereas the number of nationals registered in this sector according to the Social Security figures were only 116,000. In Italy, nationals and other EU15 domestic workers amounted to 274,000, whereas Italians registered as such in the Social Security were only 148,000. Despite the necessary cautions about the sources and their comparability, it is clear that the real size of the domestic sector in both countries is much larger than Social Security figures reveal, not only for immigrants but also, particularly in Spain, for natives.

The LFS data also show that in both countries female employment in the care sector at large increased more than in the general labour market. In Spain total female employment doubled between 1995 and 2008, but the growth was higher (128%) in the care sector at large, including health, care and domestic work than in the rest of the economy (91.5%). The same is true for Italy, despite more modest general growth of 40%. Here

---

3. Immediately after the end of the transition period in June 2012, the new conservative government announced that the legal reform had failed, and decided to come back to the old system in 2013.
4. Up to 2003, in Italy it was only possible to distinguish between foreign-born and native-born people.

TABLE 3. Female employment by sector of activity and origin, selected years (thousands in first row and column% in second row)

SPAIN	2008 non-EU15	2008 EU15	2006 non-EU15	2006 EU15	2003 non-EU15	2003 EU15	2000 non-EU15	2000 EU15	1995 non-EU15	1995 EU15	Growth 1995–2008 (all) %	Growth thousands
Health	6.8	411.6	10.5	376.8	4.3	308.4	2.3	248.0	0.1	189.8	120.2	228.5
	0.6	5.6	1.2	5.3	1.0	5.0	2.0	4.5	0.7	4.5		
Care	63.6	426.3	69.7	427.5	27.2	337.7	11.5	272.9	1.2	200.0	143.5	288.7
	5.5	5.8	7.8	6.0	6.2	5.5	10.1	4.9	5.8	4.7		
Domestic	511.7	800.1	371.3	753.4	214.7	728.0	49.4	701.6	12.1	572.2	124.5	727.5
	44.3	10.8	41.6	10.6	49.1	11.8	43.6	12.6	56.9	13.5		
Care sector at large	582.0	1638.0	451.5	1557.7	246.2	1374.1	63.2	1222.5	13.5	961.9	127.6	1244.6
	49.6	77.8	49.5	78.1	43.7	77.7	44.3	78.0	36.6	77.4		
Other	573.0	5746.9	441.8	5558.5	191.3	4796.6	50.2	4329.8	7.8	3292.7	91.5	3019.4
	50.4	22.2	50.5	21.9	56.3	22.3	55.7	22.0	63.4	22.6		
Total	1155.1	7384.9	893.3	7116.2	437.5	6170.7	113.4	5552.3	21.3	4254.7	99.7	4264
	100.0	100.0	100.0	100.0	100.0	100.0	100.0	100.0	100.0	100.0		

ITALY	2008 non-EU15	2008 EU15	2006 non-EU15	2006 EU15	2003 foreign-born	2003 native	2000 foreign-born	2000 native	1995 foreign-born	1995 native	% Growth 1995–2008	Thousands
Health	23.5	605.0	13.9	558.1	2.7	430.3	2.8	413.3	2.4	333.2	87.2	292.9
	3.4	6.6	2.7	5.9	1.9	5.2	3.8	5.4	5.8	4.8		
Care	49.9	249.5	42.7	260.0	9.5	208.6	3.4	176.4	1.5	150.5	96.9	147.4
	7.1	2.7	8.2	2.8	6.7	2.5	4.6	2.3	3.7	2.2		
Domestic	307.8	274.1	211.3	298.6	52.6	390.6	21.4	342.7	8.1	306.9	84.7	266.9
	44.1	3.0	40.5	3.2	37.4	4.7	29.0	4.5	19.2	4.4		
Care sector at large	381.2	1128.6	268.0	1116.7	64.8	1029.5	27.6	932.5	12.0	790.7	88.1	707.1
	45.4	87.7	48.6	88.2	53.9	87.5	62.6	87.8	71.3	88.7		
Other	317.4	8033.0	253.7	8313.3	75.8	7218.7	46.2	6701.3	29.9	6251.1	32.9	2069.4
	45.4	88.2	48.6	88.7	53.9	87.5	62.6	87.8	71.3	88.7		
Total	698.5	9161.5	521.7	9429.9	140.6	8248.3	73.8	7633.7	41.9	6981.9	40.4	2836.2
	100.0	100.0	100.0	100.0	100.0	100.0	100.0	100.0	100.0	100.0		

Source: EU-Labour Force Survey. Several years. Own elaboration.
Notes: Health sector includes ISCO 222, 223, 322, 323, 324; care includes ISCO-513; and domestic sector ISCO-913.

the female employment in the care sector at large grew by 88% against a 33% of all other sectors. If we look into the care sector we also note that the employment growth was comparable across subsectors in relative terms, with a higher percentage of the formal care sector in both countries. However, given the greater size of the domestic sector in both countries, which already counted almost 600 thousands and a bit more than 300 thousands employed women in 1995 respectively in Spain and in Italy in 1995, this is the care subsectors that has attracted the highest growth in absolute numbers in the period considered: over 700 thousand new employees in Spain and over 250 thousand in Italy (where a similar growth also interested the health sector).[5] In addition, in both countries the employment growth has been concentrated on foreign workers and, as seen above, characterised by high level of irregular work both among nationals and foreigners.

3.4. The institutionalisation of the migrant care model

LTC policies in these two countries have not been targeted neither at the socialisation of risks of dependency, nor at the creation of employment in the sector. A combination of factors has created a situation in which migrant labour plays a central role in the working of the Southern European welfare regimes, with predominantly female migrants filling roles in the low-paid and informal domestic workers, while the growth of formal care employment has been more modest. Whereas the developments described above have not been explicitly supported by public policy, they do represent a key reference point in the public policy discourse. Two aspects illustrate this. Despite not having an explicit LTC policy, the Italian national government has repeatedly treated the LTC issue as a problem related to the regulation of immigration. The second aspect has to do with the evolution of the LTC system at the local and regional level. In Italy, where no substantial new LTC policies have been introduced in the last years, the recent debate on care for older people has clearly shifted attention to the need to 'regulate' and 'qualify' the existing unregulated care market, in an attempt to include migrants in the local 'network of services'. Several regions, provinces and municipalities started providing training to migrant care workers employed by families in order to 'accredit' them, introduced cash benefits to dependant people that can (only) be used for hiring a care worker on a regular contractual basis, try to

---

5. Since the Italian Labour Force Survey is known to capture less immigrant workers it is very likely that the figures about the employment growth in the domestic sector in Italy are underestimated.

facilitate the encounter of demand and supply of care provided by domestic (predominantly migrant) workers by means of local public, or publicly funded, local agencies. These local initiatives, independently from their achievements, clearly show how the new 'care model' has rapidly undergone an institutionalisation process, and is likely to affect the current and future debates on LTC policies.

In Spain, the implementation of the new LTC policy, which allows variations between autonomous regions, has a very direct effect on the type of employment that it is supposed to be created. One could expect that the ongoing debate and the actual definition of specific measures will be greatly affected by the existence of the migrant care market. As a result, recent developments in LTC practices, namely the rise of a large care market both in Spain and in Italy, is likely to have effects not only on the development (if any) of LTC policies, but also on the employment opportunities created by this policy sector, both in terms of quantity and quality of these jobs.

4. Conclusions

It has often been argued that welfare and family are much more closely intertwined in Mediterranean countries than in any other welfare regimes. Families functioned traditionally as 'shock absorbers' while the State was not expected to intervene, but to concentrate on the protection of the heads of the family. The strong emphasis in the role of the family has not been accompanied by social policies that either materially supported the family, or strengthened its capacity to provide care for its members. Rather, the reference to the responsibilities of the family served to legitimise the provision of meagre social services, as well as to overtly justify political inaction in these areas of policies (Saraceno 2003).

While scholars were highlighting the commonalities in the institutional profiles of the Southern European countries, this regime was already showing clear signs of wear. Their traditional equilibriums formed around tripartite welfare arrangements (involving the labour market, social policies and families) became de-stabilised. At the basis of such de-stabilisation were the common external pressures (globalisation and the European integration process), and the internal challenges posed by the ageing of the population, the transformation of the domestic economic and social relations. Under these new conditions, welfare equilibriums operating under the presumption that care and domestic work would be performed by full-time housewives on an unpaid basis, can no longer be sustained.

This paper has provided an overview of the relationship between the (lack of) development of LTC policies and services, and female employment in the care sector in Southern European countries. These countries have very little or only recently developed LTC policies, mainly based on cash transfers, something that clearly reflects in the very limited development of formal jobs in the caring sector. At the same time a care market has emerged in recent years predominantly staffed by migrant (undocumented) domestic workers to cater for the needs unmet by the formal market and/or by public social services.

We offered an analysis of the policy-making environments in which possible policies might evolve in the future, and their interaction with the labour market expansion for caring activities. The existence, by now, of a large care marked with the above-mentioned characteristics represents a crucial element in this policy environment. In this respect, the paper puts forward the hypothesis that the rapid 'institutionalisation' of the 'migrant care worker model', is likely to interfere with future developments in care policies in these countries, and to produce effects, not only for older people and their families, but also on the (missed) opportunity to develop a properly regulated care sector.

References

Anttonen, A. and Sipila J. (1996) 'European social care services: Is it possible to identify models?', *Journal of European Social Policy* 6: 87–100.

Arriba González de Durana, A. and Moreno Fuentes, F. J. (2009) *El tratamiento de la dependencia en los regímenes de bienestar europeos contemporáneos*, Madrid: Imserso.

Barriga Martín, L., Brezmes Nieto, M. J., García Herrero, G. and Ramírez Navarro, J. M. (2013) 'Informe sobre el desarrollo y evaluación territorial de la Ley de Promoción de Autonomía Personal y Atención a las Personas en Situación de Dependencia', Asociación Estatal de Directores y Gerentes en Servicios Sociales, http://apeto.com/files/Dictamen_Obs_Dependencia.pdf

Boeri, T. and Perotti, R. (2002) *Meno pensioni, più welfare*, Bologna: Il Mulino.

Bonoli, G. (2007) 'Time matters: Postindustrialization, new social risks, welfare state adaptation in advanced industrial democracies', *Comparative Political Studies* 40(5): 495–520.

Brennan, D., Cass, B., Himmelweit, S. and Szebehely, M. (2012) 'The marketisation of care: Rationales and consequences in Nordic and liberal care regimes', *Journal of European Social Policy* 22(4): 377–91.

Cebolla, H. and González-Ferrer, A. (2008) *La inmigración en España (2000–2007). De la gestión de flujos a la integración de los inmigrantes*, Madrid: CEPC.

Cebolla, H. and González-Ferrer, A. (2013) *Cómo se ha gestionado la inmigración en España*, Madrid: Alianza Editorial.

Colombo, A. (2003) 'Razza, genere, classe: Tre dimensioni del lavoro domestico in Italia', *Polis* XVII(2): 317–42.

Costa-Font, J. and Garcia Gonzalez, A. (2007) 'Long term care reform in Spain', *Eurohealth* 13(1): 20–2.

Da Roit, B. (2006) 'La riforma dell'indennità di accompagnamento', in C. Gori (ed.), *La riforma dell'assistenza ai non autosufficienti*, Bologna: Milano, pp. 287–315.

Da Roit, B. (2010) *Care Strategies. Changing Elderly Care in Italy and the Netherlands*, Amsterdam: University Press.

Da Roit, B. (2012) 'The Netherlands: the struggle between universalism and cost containment', *Health and Social Care in the Community* 20(3): 228–37.

Da Roit, B. and Le Bihan, B. (2010) 'Similar and yet so different: Cash-for-care in six European countries' long-term care policies', *Milbank Quarterly* 88(3): 286–309.

Da Roit, B. and Sabatinelli, S. (2005) 'Il modello mediterraneo di welfare tra famiglia e mercato', *Stato e Mercato* 74(2): 267–90.

Da Roit, B. and Sabatinelli, S. (2012) 'Nothing on the move or just going private? Understanding the freeze on child- and eldercare policies and the development of care markets in Italy', *Social Politics*. doi:10.1093/sp/jxs023. Early view.

Da Roit, B. and Weicht, B. (2013) 'Migrant care work and care, migration and employment regimes: a fuzzy-set analysis', *Journal of European Social Policy* 23(5): doi:10.1177/0958928713499175

Folbre, N. and Nelson, J. A. (2000) 'For love or money – or both?', *The Journal of Economic Perspectives* 14(4): 123–40.

Haberkern, K. and Szydlik, M. (2010) 'State care provision, societal opinion and children's care of older parents in 11 European countries', *Ageing & Society* 30: 299–323.

Kolberg, J. E. (ed.). (1991) *The Welfare State as Employer*, London: M. E. Sharpe.

Esping-Andersen, G. (1990) *The Three Worlds of Welfare Capitalism*, Cambridge: Polity Press.

Esping-Andersen, G. (1999) *The Social Foundations of Postindustrial Economies*, Oxford: Oxford University Press.

McGregor, M. J., Cohen, M., McGrail, K., Broemeling, A. M., Adler, R. N., Schulzer, M., Ronald, L., Cvitkovich, Y. and Beck, M. (2005) 'Staffing levels in not-for-profit and for-profit long-term care facilities:

Does type of ownership matter?', *Canadian Medical Association Journal* 172(5): 645–9.

Meagher, G. and Cortis, N. (2009) 'The political economy of for-profit paid care: Theory and evidence', in D. King and G. Meagher (eds), *Paid Care in Australia: Politics, Profits, Practices*, Sydney: Sydney University Press, pp. 13–42.

Meil, G. (2011) *Individualización y solidaridad familiar*, Barcelona: Colección Estudios Sociales La Caixa, n° 32.

Mesini, D., Pasquinelli, S., and Rusmini, G. (2006) *Il lavoro privato di cura in Lombardia. Caratteristiche e tendenze in materia di qualificazione e regolarizzazione*, Milano: Rapporto di ricerca Irs.

Millar, J. and Warman, A. (1996) *Family obligations in Europe*, London: Family Policy Studies Centre.

Naldini, M. and Saraceno, C. (2008) 'Social and family policies in Italy: Not frozen but far from structural reforms', *Social Policy and Administration* 42(7): 733–48.

Pavolini, E. and Ranci, C. (2008) 'Restructuring the welfare state: Reforms in long-term care in Western European countries', *Journal of European Social Policy* 18(3): 246–59.

Pfau-Effinger, B. and Rostgaard, T. (2011) *Care Between Work and Welfare in European Societies*, Houndmills, Basingstoke: Palgrave Macmillan.

Ranci, C., Da Roit, B. and Pavolini, E. (2008) 'Partire dall'esistente: le caratteristiche dell'indennità di accompagnamento e alcune proposte di riforma', in C. Ranci (ed.), *Tutelare la non autosufficienza. Una proposta di riforma dell'indennitá di accompagnamento*, Roma: Carocci, pp. 9–37.

Reyneri, E. (2003) *Sociologia del mercato del lavoro*, Bologna: Mulino.

Reyneri, E. (2001) *Migrants' Involvement in Irregular Employment in the Mediterranean Countries of the European Union*, Geneva: International Labour Office.

Rosenau, P. and Linder, S. H. (2003) 'Two decades of research comparing for-profit and non-profit health provider performance in the United States', *Social Science Quarterly* 84(2): 219–41.

Saraceno, C. (2003) *Mutamenti della famiglia e politiche sociali in Italia*, Bologna: Il Mulino.

Saraceno, C. and Naldini, M. (2007) *Sociologia della famiglia*, Bologna: Il Mulino.

Sarasa, S. (2011) 'Long-term care: The persistence of familialism', in A. M. Guillén and M. León (eds), *The Spanish Welfare State in European Context*, London: Ashgate, pp. 237–58.

Simonazzi, A. (2009) 'Care regimes and national employment models', *Cambridge Journal of Economics* 33(2): 211–32.

Szebehely, M. and Trydegård, G.-B. (2011) 'Home care in Sweden: A Universal Model in transition', *Health & Social Care in the Community* 20(3): 300–9.

Taylor-Gooby, P. (2004) 'New risk and social change', in P. Taylor-Gooby (ed.), *New Risk, New Welfare: The Transformation of the European Welfare*, Oxford: Oxford University Press, pp. 1–28.

Trydegard, G. B. (2003) 'Swedish care reforms in the 1990s: A first evaluation of their consequences for the elderly people', *Revue française des affaires sociales* 4: 443–60.

IS SOCIAL PROTECTION IN GREECE AT A CROSSROADS?

Maria Petmesidou

Department of Social Administration and Political Science, Democritus University of Thrace, Greece

ABSTRACT: This paper critically examines the limitations and deadlocks of welfare patterns embedded in the statist-familialist regime that for a long-time has been pivotal for the institutional set up and processes of social redistribution in Greece. Changes to social protection under the combined effect of conflicts and impasses of this regime, and of an intractable sovereign debt crisis (largely due to accumulated deadlocks) that has engulfed the country since the late 2000s are our main focus. Current welfare reforms across major policy areas are examined, with the aim to foreshadow the direction of impending change; and, particularly, to trace any indications of whether reform can bolster 'inclusive solidarity' and improve redistribution or, instead, will bring about heightened insecurity.

1. Introduction[1]

Much of the debate on South European (SE) welfare states over the last decade focused on their imbalances and, particularly, on their pension bias crowding out resources for support to families at earlier stages of the life cycle, undeveloped social safety nets, high labour market segmentation, and great inequalities in social insurance coverage. The need for remodelling institutional arrangements and the financial mix for social protection in these countries was repeatedly stressed in the academic debate primarily with an emphasis on scaling down 'peaks of generosity' and balancing protection across a wide range of labour market 'insider' and 'outsider' groups (see, among others, the contributions to the volume

---

1. This is a research paper written in the context of the CABISE project (Capitalismo de bienestar en el sur de Europa: una evaluación comparada), under the 'Plan Nacional de I + D + i, Spain' (programme code CSO2012-33976). A first draft was presented at the 19th International Conference of Europeanists, in Boston Mass., 22–24 March 2012.

edited by Ferrera 2005; and Petmesidou 2006a). The present crisis puts into starker relief the predicaments of SE social protection systems and, undoubtedly, constitutes a watershed moment for social welfare.

The first part of the paper critically discusses the deadlocks and crisis effects of a social welfare model (for a long-time prevailing in Greece) that combined rent-seeking statist practices with a 'male breadwinner/familialist regime'. The second part brings into focus the reform dynamics under the current conjuncture of a severe economic and financial crisis expected to have protracted knock-on effects on the Greek society and economy. Central to our analysis are the strains exerted by the sovereign debt crunch on major social policy areas such as pensions, health and social care.

The article concludes with a view of where structural adjustment is heading to. The vital question at issue is whether the current reform wave can effectively address social needs and promote 'inclusive solidarity'. Or, alternatively a bleak scenario of deepening social polarisation, heightened insecurity among large sections of the population and increasing dependency on a seriously debilitated welfare state will prevail.

2. The rent-seeking statist model, unmet social need and the eruption of the sovereign debt crisis

Greece is facing the worst economic crisis since World War II. The sovereign debt crunch that emerged in 2009 (excessively high public deficit and debt levels disclosed after the revision of the budget gap) undermined the credibility of the country and led to escalating borrowing costs, bringing the economy near bankruptcy.[2]

In March 2010, a bailout loan package was agreed between Greece and the EU-ECB-IMF (the so-called 'troika') with the aim to cover the country's borrowing requirements for the next three years. Strict austerity measures were attached to it, in parallel with structural changes in the economy and public administration. However, in the two years following the 'rescue deal', the economy remained stuck into deep recession (GDP contracted by about 22% from 2008 to 2012 and is estimated to further plunge by nearly 5% in 2013), unemployment soared (reaching 26.8% in May 2013, the highest rate in the EU[3]), while social unrest escalated. The

2. Major macroeconomic parameters of the crisis (among others, inherent flaws of the Euro project, persistently bad public finances and other systemic defects of Greece's economy) are outside the scope of our analysis.

3. Youth unemployment jumped to a record high of 59.2%. Unless otherwise stated, statistics are taken from the web pages of either Elstat at http://www.statistics.gr or Eurostat at http://epp.eurostat.ec.europa.eu/portal/page/portal/eurostat/home/ (last update 30-05-2013).

alarmingly deepening crisis brought into relief that many of the assumptions embraced into the initial bailout plan for Greece's debt sustainability were problematic. A revision of the rescue programme in July 2011 (encompassing a 21% write-down on the face value of the bonds held by private bondholders) was soon considered by the international lenders not sufficient for stabilising the debt dynamics. A third iteration of the plan was agreed in late October 2011 for a fresh loan of 130bn Euros, in parallel with a 50% debt restructuring for private bondholders, with strict conditionalities exacting swingeing budgetary cuts, labour market deregulation, drastic public employment reduction and other structural reforms. Strikingly, a few months after the 'haircut' operation, and as soon as a shaky government coalition was formed, after two successive national elections (in May and June 2012), forecasts of a ballooning, unsustainable debt triggered a new round of programme revision. Deeper cuts to pensions, salaries and other expenses and further deregulation accompanied the fourth bailout iteration (of late November 2012) amidst persistent uncertainty though as to the viability of the plan.

Rising social spending prior to the crisis is considered among the factors contributing to it, as though the welfare state in Greece had grown to its limits (Matsaganis 2011). Indeed social spending rapidly increased over the last three decades, and surely profligate borrowing by successive governments (combined with EU funding flowing into the country) significantly boosted expenses. However some cautionary remarks need to be made. Greece started from a comparatively low-spending level in the early 1980s (around 12% of GDP) and before the outbreak of the crisis still lagged behind the EU-15 social spending average (24.7% in 2007, compared to 26.7% in the EU-15). Notably, even though per capita GDP in Greece converged to the EU-15 average, reaching about 90% in 2008, per capita social expenditure hardly surpassed 80% of the respective EU-15 rate. Also, employment in public social services has persistently been comparatively low (11% in 2008, compared to 15% in the EU-15[4]). These findings run counter to the 'growth to the limits' argument and rather indicate that the country under-spent in social protection in terms of its wealth. Closely linked to this is the very low level of state revenues in Greece (37% of GDP in 2008, compared to EU-15 average of 44%) and the highly regressive fiscal policy pursued, given extensive reliance on indirect taxes and the persistently huge tax evasion particularly from the well-off groups.[5] These conditions put limits to welfare state funding and

---

4. And about a quarter in Sweden, a high social spending country.
5. Indirect taxes amount to about 60% of total tax revenue; tax dodging is around 5bn Euros a year, while the informal economy is estimated to about 30% of GDP (Vassardani 2011).

hardly favoured a politics of solidarity on collective welfare that could secure the support of a wide range of social strata (principally in the middle and upper middle ranks) for redistribution. Instead a configuration of rent-seeking statist-clientelistic structures and practices dominated socio-political integration for a long-time, making access by households, individuals and businesses to 'political credentials' a central means for the appropriation of resources and fostering a perception of social problems in individualist/familist terms. This is closely linked with a welfare pattern in which the family has traditionally played a crucial role in pooling resources (from various sources, e.g. the formal and informal labour market, welfare benefits, access to public employment and others) and providing support at times of hardship, as well as care services, to its members (Petmesidou 2006a).

Given the fact that social protection evolved around a Bismarckian social insurance model (but a greatly fragmented one), it is evident that it centres upon a male breadwinner component, though it represents a weak variation of this model. Income maintenance accruing to the male breadwinner has not been sufficient to cater for family welfare needs. Striking evidence concerns the comparatively low redistributive effect of social benefits and the persistently high poverty levels in Greece even before the crisis (Dafermos and Papatheodorou 2011). Equally deficient have been family policy (with very meagre family benefits) and other related policy fields (such as housing policy), even though the family is a main welfare provider. Statutory support to the family was substituted by an institutional configuration firmly linking a rent-providing statist model with 'soft-budgeting' practices pursued by individuals, families and enterprises that allowed budget imbalances to be transferred to the state through strategies of income appropriation by political means (that is, on the basis of access to clientelist poles of power). Within this framework, competition for the control of the 'revenue yielding mechanisms of state power' was paramount, creating a crucial dimension of social inequality (and social exclusion, for those groups unable to secure legitimate political credentials of access to state power), intertwined with inequalities based on market power. Needless to say such a mode of socio-political integration hardly favoured a social citizenship view of universalist welfare.

Reviewing briefly the welfare state effort in Greece, the following points can be made. First, as in the other SE countries, public responsibility for social welfare took off at a time (early 1980s) when the welfare states in North-West Europe came under pressure in the face of growing fiscal problems, new social risks, and a neo-liberal politico-ideological orientation that severely affected welfare state legitimacy (particularly in the Anglo-Saxon countries). Second, enactment of social rights and social programmes (e.g. implementation of a national health system) occurred in a much shorter time period compared to North-West Europe, a condition accounting for weak consolidation of new institutions. Soon fiscal constraints became highly pressing, particularly under the project of Greece's joining the European Monetary Union and the subsequent fiscal discipline requirements of the Stability Pact. Expansionary trends slowed down and an urgent need for welfare state retrenchment emerged, even though the welfare state hardly reached a level of maturity compared to North-West Europe (Guillén and Petmesidou 2008; Petmesidou 2013).

Third, a 'hybrid' welfare model was sustained under these conditions. Income transfers (mostly pensions, developed along occupational lines) have persistently been its major component. More than any other SE country, Greece developed a highly fragmented and polarised system with wide imbalances among the 130 social insurance funds in existence until recently. In the early 1980s, a social-democratic element was introduced with the establishment of a National Health System (NHS), indicating a path shift that, however, remained incomplete (private health expenditure kept growing and multiple health funds with inequalities in coverage continued to operate). As to social care services and social assistance, these have traditionally been a residual element of social protection based on means-testing, a characteristic that indicates a liberal orientation. Overall, the impact of welfare state interventions has persistently been very limited in reducing inequality, as is testified by the comparatively high Gini coefficient (0.343; EU–15 average 0.302, in 2007).

At the onset of the crisis, extreme fragmentation and polarisation in social insurance, swelling administrative costs and accumulated incentives for early retirement, in combination with rapid demographic ageing and negative economic growth hiked pension expenditure to over 13% of GDP (expected to nearly double by 2050). A reform enacted in 2008, with the ambitious aim to improve administrative efficiency by drastically reducing the number of social funds (from 130 to 13), masked the preservation of the system's complex structure, as the numerous constituent units of the new fund configurations retained their distinctive characteristics and regulations. Hence major predicaments remained, necessitating a wholesale reform for securing long-term sustainability of pensions; harmonising regulations across the numerous funds; achieving transparency of budget allocation (for instance, by clearly distinguishing between insurance and social assistance, as well as by separating pension funds from health insurance funds); and effectively tackling poverty among the elderly.

Equally, total health care spending grew steadily from about 6.5% of GDP at the time of the introduction of the NHS, in 1981, to about 9% in late 2000s. However, private expenditure has persistently been high, amounting to 40% of total health spending. It consists of out-of-pocket payments (according to OECD data, in mid to late 2000s, these stood well above 90% of total private health expenditure). Extensive reliance on out-of-pocket payments (part of it being under-the-table payments) and indirect taxation (by the mid 2000s about a fifth of total health expenditure was financed by taxation, with indirect taxes accounting for a large part of it) renders the system highly regressive (among others, see Davaki and Mossialos 2006; Petmesidou and Guillén 2008; Siskou *et al.* 2008). Furthermore, historically, the main obstacles to building a truly national health system in Greece were a serious lack of support by major social actors, conflicting interests within the medical community, discretionary privileges of particular social insurance funds, and complex ties between the public and private sector fostering corruption and waste of resources.

Social services are poorly developed and informal care within the family is key for meeting needs (Petmesidou 2006b). Growing demand for care due to changes in demography, family patterns and gender roles has progressively been met by female migrant labour (either as co-residing or day-care minders, Guillén and Petmesidou 2008: 75). An informal privatisation pattern thus emerged where the family still plays a coordinating role but care tasks are undertaken by foreign minders. Such arrangements, however, turn to be highly fragile under the impact of the economic crisis. Increasing hardship makes difficult for households to afford a paid caretaker and strongly exacerbates the need for a new framework for sharing of public/private responsibility in social care.

Notably, well before the onset of the crisis, there was extensive unmet need, as the above welfare pattern for a long-time sustained a divide between some fairly well protected social groups (enjoying access to the formal labour market and clientelistic networks), and a number of deprived social groups (the precariously employed, particularly in the underground economy; old-age people with no rights to social insurance or with insufficient coverage; unqualified young persons; the long-term unemployed and others). At the current conjuncture the critical question is whether the crisis can offer a window of opportunity for redressing the insider/outsider divide and widening the scope of institutionalised rights (e.g. by introducing a universal minimum income guarantee and the right to protection by the frail and dependent persons). Or, instead, cost-containment will be a downwards equalising attempt to a common low denominator, with detrimental effects on large sections of the population. While the verdict is still out, indications abound that the latter option may prevail.

3. Austerity and the future of the welfare state

Largely, under the bailout agreement, the main policy options embrace drastic falls in wages and salaries,[6] significant hikes in indirect taxes[7] and special levies[8] that hit disproportionally low and middle-income earners; and considerable cuts in current and future pension entitlements, and social assistance benefits (a weak, anyway, element of income maintenance).

Markedly, in 2011, a tax reform significantly reduced the lowest taxable yearly income from 12,000 to 5000 Euros (that is, below the poverty line set at about 550 Euros for a single person at that time), and the new tax rates placed a disproportionately heavy burden on low to middle incomes (up to 35,000 Euros yearly; Kada 2011). Under the pressure of achieving budget compliance in the upcoming years, the tax reform agenda opened once more in late 2012. New legislation further extended the tax base to factor in low-income groups, and abolished tax breaks and allowances (hurting particularly low- to middle-income families with children). These are regressive measures severely squeezing Greece's already austerity-hit lower and middle class.

Harsh cuts in public health expenditure are prominent on the reform agenda too. These are pursued through merging (closing down) hospitals, applying e-procurement for generics and shifting the cost to the 'consumer' (by increasing private provision within the NHS and cutting the range of services covered under public health care). As to care services, persistent reliance on EU sources of funding and precariousness of employment for much of the staff (as hirings have been mostly on a temporary basis in programmes such as 'home help' and 'day-care') contribute to making them easy victims of austerity measures.

---

6. The purchasing power of average wage and salary earnings dropped by 50% in 2011–2012, as the combined result of a (on average) 23% reduction of incomes, rising prices and a tax raid (Kouzis 2012: 4). Gross average earnings are forecasted to further drop in 2013 (by over 8%, in real terms; Bank of Greece 2012).
7. On food, cigarettes, gasoline and electricity. Also, in late 2012, heating oil tax increased six-fold.
8. As for instance the (highly unpopular) 'extra' property levy introduced in 2011 as a temporary measure initially to plug a hole of 2bn Euros in the 2011 budget, but later on decided to be sustained in the following years' budgets. It is a kind of poll tax charged (through the electricity bill) to all users of property under threat of having their electricity cut. Given the rather small payment margin between old and new property, its effect on perverse redistribution is obvious. After public outcry over the unfairness of the measure a decision was taken by the government to exempt some categories of highly vulnerable groups. Recently a high court ruled that cutting off electricity for non-payment of the levy is unconstitutional.

3.1. Pension reform: Is fiscal sustainability incongruent to adequacy?

The need for rationalising a pension system ridden with inefficiencies and great inequalities in coverage, benefit level and funding is of high priority in the bailout agreement. In mid 2010 a 'pathbreaking' overhaul was approved by Parliament. This signposts a shift from a greatly fragmented, Bismarckian social insurance system (based primarily on the fist pillar), to a unified, multi-tier system that distinguishes between a basic (quasi-universal) non-contributory and a contributory pension, to be in force from January 2015. The amount of the basic pension is set at 360 Euros (but may be reduced if economic performance deteriorates), and the contributory part is linked to paid contributions. The basic pension is granted to old-aged uninsured persons (including people who paid contributions for less than 15 years) on condition that they satisfy specific requirements. The law also provides for an annual adjustment of pensions (from 2014 onwards) on the basis of a coefficient drawing on GDP fluctuations, on the consumer price index and the financial situation of pension funds.

Most importantly, as from 2015 the state's responsibility is limited to the basic pension. Henceforth, any deficits incurred by social insurance organisations should be dealt with by reducing pensions and/or increasing contributions. The government guarantee of auxiliary pensions was abolished too. The vague statement that the state guarantees the viability of the system so as to secure a decent pension for retirees, inscribed in the law in a last moment attempt by the Labour Minister to appease dissenters within the governing party, does not really alter the spirit of the reform.

Of crucial importance is system rationalisation attempted through the further amalgamation of social insurance organisations. Three major funds form the backbone of social insurance: IKA (the Social Insurance Organisation, until recently covering the majority of private sector workers, embraces public sector employees too); OAEE (the social insurance fund for self-employed workers, excluding liberal professions); and OGA (the farmers' retirement fund). Exemptions for specific categories remained, though, as the government backtracked in front of strong resistance by the trade unions of journalists and media workers, doctors, engineers and lawyers to having their funds amalgamated to OAEE.[9]

The crux of the reform boils down to significant changes in pensionable income and replacement rates. Pensionable income will be calculated on

---

9. An umbrella organisation (ETAA, the Social Insurance Fund of Independent Professionals) embraced the social insurance schemes of liberal professions, while their administrations kept a considerable degree of autonomy.

the basis of earnings during the whole working career, rather than those of the last five years before retirement (as was the case until recently). The combination of shrinking pensionable income and a lower replacement rate will lead to significant reductions of pensions reaching progressively up to 50% for future retirees, as the new regulations will progressively come into full force from 2015 onwards (Institute of Labour 2010: 315). Stricter conditions were introduced for early retirement as well as for pensioners who continue working; measures were taken for equalising men and women's retirement conditions (in a phased-in way); and provisions were made for linking it to longevity (from 2021 onwards).[10]

An overhaul of the conditions concerning entitlement to disability is also under way, as cracking down on abuse constitutes a major aim. Yet in an attempt to drastically reduce spending on disability pensions from about 15% of total pension expenditure to 10% or even less, stricter regulations (and monitoring procedures) seriously affect also genuine cases of disability with significant rolling-back of provisions.[11]

Under the pressure of serious fiscal woes of the country and alarming forecasts for rapidly increasing pension spending as the baby-boomer generation retires, fiscal sustainability criteria dominated policy options. Notably, the bailout agreement stipulates that the contribution of the state budget to pension expenditure should not surpass an increase by 2.5 percentage points of GDP through 2060. However, this is a very unrealistic premise, unless steep decreases of pension income will take place (further to the cuts already imposed) throwing even larger numbers of elderly people into poverty.

Importantly, the sustainability argument appears to be rather controversial on various grounds. First, particularly in the medium term, a hike in the number of retirees will increase pension expenditure (by about 1.2bn Euros over the next five years, according to estimates by the Ministry of Labour and Social Insurance). Yet, gloomy future forecasts for the economy (protracted deep recession and galloping unemployment) will make revenue of social insurance funds steeply plunge[12] and, thus, will seriously detract from the viability estimates of the reform plan. Second, contributions evasion persists unabated (it currently stands at a little over a fourth of IKA's revenues and about a third of those of OAEE

10. New legislation also increased the retirement age to 67 years from January 2013.
11. In addition, a revised list of 'arduous and unhygienic' jobs, which highly reduced the number of workers enjoying specific benefits and early retirement conditions, has been into effect recently.
12. IKA lost 4.2bn Euros in 2010 and 2011, according to the ex-Minister of Labour and Social Insurance, G. Koutroumanis (accessed at http://www.tovima.gr/finance/article/?aid = 441353) and the downfall of revenue continues.

and OGA), and huge arrears in contributions payments by enterprises put severe strains on social insurance. Third, corruption scandals (as is for instance the 'structured-bonds' scandal, back in 2007, involving a number of social insurance organisations), and absence of professional management of funds have been especially damaging on sustainability and fairness accounts.[13] Furthermore, the over 50% haircut of bondholding imposed on social insurance funds under the PSI (that is, the Private Sector Involvement in a complex bond-swap programme implemented in March 2012 as part of the rescue plan) dramatically affected social insurance organisations as they wrote down losses over 12bn Euros.

Controversies concern also the harmonisation of regulations and the principle of universality in respect to the basic (flat rate) pension. Despite the aim to build a unified system and promote distributional fairness, exemptions remained for some socio-professional groups, as indicated earlier. Obviously resistance by the liberal professions to the merging of their distinct social funds with OAEE is accounted for by reasonable worries that such a reform would drag entitlements downwards for their funds.

Regulations for the provision of the basic pension manifest that this is not a fully universal benefit, as old-age persons not entitled to a contributory pension must fulfil certain income criteria in order to be eligible for it. Equally controversial are the 'blurry messages' of policy in respect to early retirement (or, conversely, to 'active ageing'). On the one hand, the stated aim of the reform is to put the brake on early retirement. But, on the other hand, recent ministerial decisions facilitate early exit in the short- and medium-term for specific groups (e.g. for women aged 55 years and over with underage children and 18.5 years of work – a temporary measure that, however, led about 50,000 women to early retirement in 2010; provision of 'notional insured time' to parents and other similar regulations).[14]

Significant questions as to distributional fairness and sustainability emerge also in respect to a special (intergenerational solidarity) levy, introduced in August 2010 (ranging initially between 3% to 10% of gross monthly (basic) pension income, but raised up to 14% in early 2012,[15] in order to create a contingency fund for social insurance organisations. Contrary to the expressed aim for this levy to contribute to a pension

---

13. Not to mention the policy followed for many years in the (distant) past by Greek governments allowing them to use IKA's surpluses (with negligible return) for subsidising firms, which strongly contributed to bring IKA's finances into red in the 1980s (Petmesidou 2006a: 50).

14. The panic created by the pension reform, in parallel with drastic cuts in earnings act as strong push factors to retirement.

15. A levy to auxiliary pensions over 300 Euros monthly (ranging from 3% to 4%) was introduced in September 2011 too.

reserve fund for meeting future financial strains on social insurance, legislation passed in October 2011 in a dubious way made the Ministry of the Interior co-responsible for the administration of the resources of the reserve fund, allowing thus the use of (part of) these resources for plugging holes in the debt-stricken local authorities.[16]

Structural changes in the pension system are often of a long-term perspective, with no significant immediate impact. Nevertheless, rapid phase-in arrangements and, mostly, across the board cuts in pension incomes deal a serious blow to the living standards of large groups of present day retirees. Over 2010 and 2011 austerity measures led to about 3bn Euros cuts in pensions amounting to a reduction close to 10% of total pension expenditure. Moreover, from January 2012, gross basic pension incomes exceeding 1300 Euros monthly were reduced by 12%, and progressive cuts by 10% to 20% for auxiliary pensions (up to 250 /over 300 Euros, respectively) were introduced.[17] Income losses hurting particularly low-income pensioners were incurred, also, as a result of the abolition of 'Christmas'/'Easter' and 'Vacation' benefits, as well as of the (means-tested) 'heating benefit' provided by the National Social Cohesion Fund (established a few years ago in order to administer social assistance but abolished before becoming fully operational), and stricter targeting rules for the provision of EKAS (a social solidarity benefit). Massive cuts (by nearly 80% for some social funds) in the one-off payment to retirees dealt a further blow to pensioners' living conditions.

The most recent available data on poverty refer to 2010 incomes (EU-SILC data for 2011). Thus, they do not fully capture the effects of harsh austerity measures in the following years. Elderly people have persistently faced a higher poverty risk than the total population. A downward trend, evident prior to the crisis, has been reversed (Petmesidou forthcoming). The aggregate poverty rate rose from 20.1%[18] in 2008 (2007 incomes) to 21.4% in 2011 (2010 incomes; respective EU-27 average rates 16.3% and 16.9%); while the poverty rate for people 65 years or over rose, accordingly, from 22% to 24%. Alarmingly, the combined at-risk-of-poverty and/or social exclusion aggregate rate reached 31% (affecting 3.5 million people in Greece; EU-27 average rate 24.2%). It stood at about 34% among old-aged people (75 years or over; 36% among old-aged women).

---

16. Strikingly, the law stipulates that part of the resources of this fund can be used by cash-strapped local authorities to finance 'home help' programmes addressed (on a strict means-testing basis) to the neediest elderly people. Indeed, a policy measure that follows the trodden path in Greece of blurring insurance with social assistance.

17. Under the fourth bailout revision a further cut ranging from 5% to 20% of total gross monthly pension incomes over 1000 Euros took place in January 2013.

18. Cut-off point: 60% of the median income.

Evidently, crucial challenges remain in respect to fiscal rationalisation and distributional justice, while drastic cuts seriously aggravate poverty and deprivation among the elderly.

3.2. Rolling back health care coverage and (the even rudimentary) statutory social care

Four decades passed since the establishment of the NHS, and the system hardly reached the state of a fully fledged national health service. Both in terms of funding and service delivery a mixed system continued to operate until recently: an occupation-based health insurance system, combined with a national health service, in parallel with expanding private provision. Soaring hospital deficits over the last decade, persistent fragmentation of health insurance and inequalities in the scope of coverage, as well as lack of coordination between primary and secondary care were the main predicaments. The bursting of the public debt bubble made system rationalisation a key priority. However, how far, in the context of harsh cuts, a balance between efficiency and fairness can be achieved remains an open question. Particularly in the case of social care, spiralling budgetary pressures over the last couple of years seriously threaten even the so far rudimentary provision.

Strikingly, despite comparatively high (total) health expenditure, life expectancy over the last decade rose by only one and a half year, indicating a limited effectiveness of health care. Most importantly, a difference of about 16 years for women and 12 years for men between life expectancy and healthy life years (at birth)[19] indicates a bad health status for old-aged people and, particularly, for old-aged women.

Moreover, as indicated by the EU–SILC data on 'self-reported health status' (Table 1), even before the crisis had fully stricken, inequalities in respect to people with 'very bad' health status manifested a deepening trend. The gap between the top- and mid-income quintile significantly increased, as the percentage of people in the latter quintile, who perceive their health status as 'very bad' rose rapidly over the second half of the 2000s; and the gap between the top- and bottom-income quintile only slightly decreased. These findings contrast with trends in other SE countries (e.g. Spain, where an improvement is recorded in the second half of the 2000s).

Poorly developed public (and preventive) health care policies partly account for these conditions. The deepening economic crisis is forecasted

---

19. 82.7 and 66.8 years respectively for women; 77.8 and 66.1 years respectively for men (in 2009).

TABLE 1.   Indicators of health status and social care needs

		2 0 0 5			2 0 1 1		
		Bottom income quintile* (%)	Mid income quintile* (%)	Top income quintile* (%)	Bottom income quintile* (%)	Mid income quintile* (%)	Top income quintile* (%)
Self-perceived	Greece	4.1	2.3	0.8	3.5	3.1	0.9
'very bad'	Spain	4.3	2.6	0.8	2.4	2.3	0.9
health status	Portugal	10.6	5.4	1.7	8.4	5.5	1.9
(total	Italy	2.3	1.8	1.2	2.6	2.2	0.9
population)	*Sweden*	*3.1*	*0.8*	*0.5*	*2.4*	*0.7*	*0.3*
	EU-27	*4.2*	*1.7*	*0.8*	*3.0*	*1.8*	*0.7*
Self-perceived	Greece	9.1	6.0	2.6	11.5	9.9	3.7
limitations in	Spain	13.0	9.2	5.5	5.6	5.7	3.0
daily	Portugal	20.9	11.5	5.5	14.9	9.3	4.3
activities***	Italy	8.1	6.5	3.8	6.6**	7.6**	3.7**
(total	*Sweden*	*17.7*	*10.1*	*6.5*	*11.7*	*5.9*	*2.7*
population)	*EU-27*	*8.4*	*9.1*	*4.7*	*8.6**￼*	*10.0**￼*	*4.8**￼*

Source: http://epp.eurostat.ec.europa.eu/portal/page/portal/eurostat/home/ [Sweden is included for comparison, as a high social spending country].
*   Of equivalised household income (income data refer to previous year).
**   2010 data.
***   People 'severely hampered' in their daily activities for at least the last six months.

to have further negative effects on the health status of the population (Kentikelenis *et al.* 2011). Available studies also indicate adverse effects of financial strain on mental health (reflected on a 40% increase of the annual suicide rate; Economou *et al.* 2011). Demand for public health services has significantly risen (by about 35% since 2009, according to the Ministry of Health). Yet, dramatic cuts in public health-care spending (over 40% between 2009 and 2013), shrinking number of beds (even in intensive care units), decreasing public health personnel and roll-back of coverage do not augur well for meeting rising demand for public provision.

A major predicament of the NHS has repeatedly been the accumulation of huge hospital arrears and unpaid bills.[20] In June 2010 the outstanding deficit by public hospitals (for the period 2005–2009) amounted to about 5bn Euros. Bitter conflicts with medical equipment suppliers, drug makers and pharmacists often lead to deadlocks and boycotts imposed on procurement. These cause serious shortages of essential items in the public hospital system that obstruct medical treatment and in certain cases

---

20. A steep increase characterises also pharmaceuticals expenditure by social insurance organizations. According to the Ministry of Labour and Social Insurance, from 2000 to 2009 drugs expenditure rose by 400% in IKA (from 583m to 2.4bn Euros) and by 450% (from 279m to 1.2bn Euros) in OGA.

put patients' lives at risk. Despite the deal reached with suppliers about three years ago[21] and cost-containment measures following the outbreak of the crisis, in late 2011 new outstanding hospital debt for medical supplies reached 1.1bn Euros, and for pharmaceutical bills (by hospitals and social insurance funds) 1.2bn Euros.

Legal changes enacted over the last few years provide for the all day operation of hospitals and health centres and the charging of fees per visit in the afternoon shift to outpatients (covered only partly by social insurance); the enforcement of a 5 Euros fee for all (regular) outpatient services;[22] a new drug-pricing system that sets the price of drugs on the basis of the average of the three lowest-priced markets in the EU; in parallel with the phased introduction of e-prescribing for social insurance funds, the greater penetration of generics, electronic auction for hospital supplies and systematic accounting and auditing techniques at hospitals.[23] Undoubtedly, because of considerable technical complexities in the health sector, pressures and intense conflicts due to high stakes (often producing collusion of interests nurturing corruption), and multiple, simultaneous changes attempted, a considerable time span is needed for reforms to yield results and be assessed for effectiveness.

Nevertheless, so far it is evident that fiscal concerns predominate in policy reform overshadowing any other issues and priorities (e.g. quality, equity and access criteria). Huge savings (amounting even up to 90% cuts in spending, according to the Ministry of Health) in the procurement of drastic substances and less expensive generics and medical consumables have been strongly contested by the Federation of NHS Medical Doctors' Associations on the ground of compromising quality.[24]

In a similar vein, the attempt by the government to amalgamate health insurance funds into a unified organisation – EOPYY, the 'National Health Services Organisation' – has been hotly debated by relevant stakeholders. A thorny issue is how out of some 'ailing' health insurance funds, and with diminishing resources, quality of service provision will be secured. Strikingly, a report by the Health Experts Committee submitted to the Minister of Health about three years ago warned that the planned 0.6% of (a rapidly diminishing) GDP as a subsidy to EOPYY is negligible, when, only for IKA, the subsidy (for health insurance) amounted to 1.2% of GDP prior to the amalgamation.[25] Moreover, the creation of one more

---

21. Providing for an upfront payment in cash of part of the debt, while for the remainder zero coupon bonds were offered.
22. A 25 Euros fee per hospital admission will also be in force from January 2014.
23. Piloting of Diagnosis-Related-Groups led to costly results prompting reconsideration.
24. See Newspaper 'Avgi', 15 November 2011, accessed at http://www.avgi.gr/.
25. See Newspaper 'Eleftherotypia' 19 April 2011, accessed at http://www.enet.gr/.

national health organisation, EOPYY (in parallel to the NHS), with a hybrid form – namely a funding agency (for both primary and hospital care) but also a provider of primary care services – raises problems for system rationalisation. Alternatively, making EOPYY a single funding agency for public health care, and transferring and reorganising all primary care provision under the NHS would be a step forward to better planning and allocation of resources.

Organisational and administrative reform of the NHS is also high on the agenda through the amalgamation or even the closing down of clinics and hospitals. Administrative staff shortages are intensifying due, among others, to the policy of layoffs with the aim to considerably shrink the public sector in the coming years. In addition the shortage of physicians (because of retirements and the drastic slowdown of recruitment) and, particularly, of nursing staff seriously affects service delivery.[26]

Equally important is rising employment flexibilisation of medical personnel in EOPYY health units. Medical associations repeatedly expressed worries, also, about a bleak scenario of 'a sort of medical sweatshop' with medical companies creating primary care franchises in which 'a plethora of unemployed Greek medical doctors will work for a minimum wage'.

Markedly, a new front of mobilisation of medical staff is closely linked with the 'non-payment movement' gathering momentum in Greece over the last three years (where people refuse to pay highway tolls, extra levies and public transport tickets, expressing thus their indignation about sharp rising rates and ad hoc taxes). In public hospitals this new front of mobilisation concerns the 'entrance coupon' for all regular visits to outpatient hospital departments. It consists in the occupation of cashier's office by medical staff so as to allow patients free entrance.

It is too early to pass judgement on a reform that is in progress amidst serious sovereign debt problems, uncertainty and acute confrontations with stakeholders. Suffice it to say, however, that drastic cuts and deterioration of public health provision in parallel with further increasing privatisation (due to rising fees and co-payments) impact negatively on access and equity criteria, not to mention service quality which is rarely alluded to in public documents. Seemingly a drift towards rolling back public provision and levelling down quality has begun,[27] though whether this will irreversibly lead to residual protection is an open question.

---

26. In Greece there are 3.2 nurses per 1000 inhabitants, while in Sweden the respective rate is 30 and the OECD average 9.6 (Petmesidou 2011c: 23).
27. For an analysis corroborating this perspective see also Papadopoulos and Roumpakis 2012.

Statutory care services are mostly geared towards institutional care, albeit falling far short of existing needs. Developments over the last decade or so about (i.e. domiciliary care and day-care centres for frail elderly people, centres for early diagnosis of disability, counselling and vocational training to disabled citizens and other similar projects targeted to deprived vulnerable groups) have extensively relied on EU initiatives and funding. Discontinuity in financing and precarious employment conditions for much of the staff affect negatively personnel morale and service quality. Informal privatisation through service provision within the family by paid carers rapidly expanded over the last 10 to 15 years, as mentioned above. Problems abound, however, ranging from unmet need to serious burdens placed on families. Under deteriorating economic conditions the salience of a double-bind confronting women is evident, namely opportunities for full-time paid career are seriously diminishing (female unemployment reached 31% in spring 2013), while at the same time the rolling back of the even rudimentary services seriously hampers reconciliation of family care and work.[28]

Table 1 (above) clearly indicates that care needs increased over the second half of the 2000s, as the percentage of people who experience severe limitations in their daily activities significantly rose across the income hierarchy (but the gap between the top- and mid-income quintile slightly widened). Yet, private arrangements for care provision become all the more difficult as economic hardship intensifies; while the prospects for enhancing statutory provision under the 'structural adjustment plan' are rather dim.

Evidently, harsh austerity measures highly prioritise fiscal contraction with detrimental effects on the weak Greek welfare state. To this testifies also the dismantling of employment protection under the strong insistence of the international creditors. Policies already under way include: the shift towards enterprise labour contracts (or individual contracts), and the undermining of the collective negotiation process itself, by the 'troika's' insistence on the reduction, by government fiat, of the private sector minimum wage by 22%, in February 2012;[29] sub-minimum wages for youth; significant cuts in subsidies to OAED (the Greek Labour Force Employment Organisation) that will eventually cause a further drop in the unemployment benefit (in addition to the reduction from 460 to 359 Euros

---

28. Also, economic crisis conditions accentuate multigenerational living. Persistently high youth unemployment exacerbates the financial difficulties young people encounter, if they want to live independently. Hence the rise of the so-called 'boomerang generation', that is, young people moving back home for financial reasons. Under these conditions women carry a double burden, struggling to care for ailing parents, adult children and grandchildren.
29. The minimum wage is the benchmark for all higher wage rates and of the unemployment benefit.

because of the fall in the minimum wage); easing of dismissals and employment flexibilisation.[30] Hence, instead of the crisis providing an opportunity for improving social protection of the 'outsiders' (i.e. all these weakly protected social groups under the arrangements that prevailed in the past), it rather leads to the dismantling of social rights of the 'insiders', intensifying insecurity and driving down labour and welfare standards to a low common denominator.

4. Conclusion: What prospects for 'inclusive solidarity'?

All of the above trends add up to rising hardship among large sections of the population, weakening family/kin networks that fulfilled a stabilising role in social protection, diminishing opportunities predominantly for the young, and deepening insecurity in respect to employment and retirement conditions. While, in parallel, demand for social welfare provisions increases, albeit from a progressively enfeebled welfare state. In view, also, of the weak roots of a 'politics of solidarity' in the past and recent history of the Greek social protection system – that could encourage buy-in from a wide range of middle-class strata into universalist welfare-, what are the prospects of collective welfare under structural adjustment?

In an attempt to briefly layout the contours of an answer to this question – given the rapidly changing conditions – of crucial importance is whether the structural adjustment measures will have lasting negative effects on the living standards not only of the most vulnerable social groups but also of large sections of the middle class. Even though there are not yet sufficient quantitative data on these issues, anecdotal evidence available from NGOs, mass media and other sources report that an even greater number of households in Greece (as also in the other SE countries) that until recently considered themselves as middle class with great difficulty can make ends meet (even more Greeks, Portuguese and Spaniards turn to food banks and seek help to get by, because they lost their job, went bankrupt, or had their home repossessed due to mortgage arrears; Petmesidou 2011a).

Clinging to neo-liberal recipes of swingeing austerity will bring protracted recession, increasing unemployment and economic hardship. Under these conditions a considerable number of middle-class households will sink into deprivation (and poverty), as large numbers of the self-employed, small businesses and the salaried (mostly of the public, but also,

---

30. According to information from the Labour Inspectorate, in 2011, full-time contracts were reduced by about one fifth, while part-time contracts and job rotation significantly increased; and these trends continue.

of the private sector) will be decimated by structural adjustment and protracted economic downturn. Eventually, under the emerging socio-economic reconfiguration the gap will deepen between some upper sections of the middle strata that will comfortably increase their economic and socio-political resources and a large spectrum of socio-occupational groups progressively losing ground (Petmesidou 2011a, b). Such an alarming scenario of large and rigid social gaps leaves little room for optimism for a politics of solidarity, which, as the history of the social-democratic welfare state shows, requires the existence and support of a large, cohesive middle class. It is a highly probable development, though, as the European integration project seems to be crumbling causing serious doubts about the future of the European Social Model.

References

Bank of Greece (2012) *Interim Report on Monetary Policy*, Athens: Bank of Greece (in Greek).
Dafermos, J. and Papatheodorou, C. (2011) 'The paradox of social policy in Greece: Why the increase of social expenditure has not reduced poverty', Policy Paper, Observatory on Poverty, Incomes and Social Inequalities, INE-GSEE, http://www.ineobservatory.gr/sitefiles/books/pdf/report2.pdf (in Greek).
Davaki, K. and Mossialos, E. (2006) 'Financing and delivering health care', in M. Petmesidou and E. Mossialos (eds), *Social Policy Developments in Greece*, Aldershot: Ashgate, pp. 286–318.
Economou, M., Madianos, M., Theleretis, C., Peppou, L. and Stefanis, C. (2011) 'Increased suicidality amid economic crisis in Greece', *The Lancet* 378: 1459, http://www.thelancet.com/journals/lancet/article/PIIS0140-6736(11)61638-3/fulltext
Ferrera, M. (ed.) (2005) *Welfare State Reform in Southern Europe*, London: Routledge.
Guillén, A. and Petmesidou, M. (2008) 'The private-public mix in Southern Europe. What changed in the last decade?', in M. Seeleib-Kaiser (ed.), *Welfare State Transformations*, London: Macmillan, pp. 56–78.
Institute of Labour (2010) *The Greek Economy and Employment: Annual Review*, Athens: INE-GSEE.
Kada, D. (2011) 'For €15,000 an extra tax of €700. For €200,000 the extra burden amounts to €800', Newspaper *"Eleftherotypia"* 8 October, pp. 20–21 (in Greek).
Kentikelenis, A., Karanikolos, M., Papanicolas, I., Basu, S., McKee, M. and Stuckler, D. (2011) 'Health effects of financial crisis: Omens of a

Greek tragedy', *The Lancet* 378: 1457–1458, http://www.thelancet. com/journals/lancet/article/PIIS0140-6736(11)61556-0/fulltext

Kouzis, G. (2012) 'Remarks on industrial relations measures', *Enimerosi* (Newsletter of the Labour Institute of the General Confederation of Greek Labour) 199: 2–9.

Matsaganis, M. (2011) 'The welfare state and the crisis: The case of Greece', *Journal of European Social Policy* 21(5): 501–12.

Papadopoulos, T. and Roumpakis, A. (2012) 'The Greek welfare state in the age of austerity: Anti-social policy and the politico-economic crisis', in M. Kilkey, G. Ramia and K. Farnsworth (eds), *Social Policy Review 24: Analysis and Debate in Social Policy*, Bristol: Policy Press, pp. 205–30.

Petmesidou, M. (2006a) 'Tracking social protection: Origins, path peculiarity, impasses and prospects', in M. Petmesidou and E. Mossialos (eds), *Social Policy Developments in Greece*, Aldershot: Ashgate, pp. 25–54.

Petmesidou, M. (2006b) 'Social care services: "Catching up" amidst high fragmentation and poor initiatives for change', in M. Petmesidou and E. Mossialos (eds), *Social Policy Developments in Greece*, Aldershot: Ashgate, pp. 318–57.

Petmesidou, M. (2011a) 'What future for the middle classes and "inclusive solidarity" in South Europe (a note)', *Global Social Policy* 11(2–3): 225–7.

Petmesidou, M. (2011b) 'The crisis, the middle classes and social welfare in Greece', paper presented at the SEESOX International Conference on Greece (*"Whose Crisis? Impact on Greek Politics, Economics, Society and Culture"*), St. Antony's College Oxford, May 27–28, http://www.sant. ox.ac.uk/seesox/whosecrisisarticles%20and%20papers.html

Petmesidou, M. (2011c) 'Annual Report on Greece: Pensions, health and long-term care', ASISP Network, European Commission, http://www. socialprotection.eu/files_db/1109/asisp_ANR11_Greece.pdf

Petmesidou, M. (2013) 'Southern Europe', in B. Greve (ed.), *International Handbook of the Welfare State*, London: Routledge, pp. 183–92.

Petmesidou, M. (forthcoming) 'Is the crisis a watershed moment for the Greek welfare state? The chances for modernization amidst an ambivalent EU record on "Social Europe"', in A. Triantafyllidou, R. Gropas and H. Kouki (eds), *The Greek Crisis: An Inquiry into Greek and European Modernity*, London: Palgrave.

Petmesidou, M. and Guillén, A. (2008) '"Southern style" national health services? Recent reforms and trends in Spain and Greece', *Social Policy and Administration* 42(2): 106–24.

Siskou, O., Kaitelidou, D., Papakonstantinou, V. and Liaropoulos, L. (2008) 'Private health expenditure in the Greek health care system', *Health Policy* 88(2–3): 282–93.

Vassardani, M. (2011) 'Tax evasion in Greece: A general overview', *Bank of Greece. Economic Bulletin* 35: 15–26 (in Greek).

FEMALE EMPLOYMENT AND THE ECONOMIC CRISIS

Social change in Northern and Southern Italy

Alberta Andreotti and Enzo Mingione
Department of Sociology and Social Research, University of Milano-Bicocca, Milano, Italy
Jonathan Pratschke
Department of of Economics and Statistics, University of Salerno, Salerno, Italy

ABSTRACT: One of the characteristics of the Italian peninsula is a sharp North-South gradient on many economic and labour market variables. This gradient is particularly marked in relation to female employment, making Italy a particularly useful 'laboratory' for studying changes in gender roles. Esping-Andersen's description of the decline of the 'male breadwinner' model and the search for a 'new equilibrium' in gender roles is suggestive, but the assumption that current processes will inevitably converge towards a relatively homogeneous social configuration (exemplified by the Scandinavian countries) is rather unconvincing. We will show in this article that the Italian case comprises macro-regions with very different female employment rates and highly differentiated welfare systems. Furthermore, one of the effects of the economic crisis has been to obstruct the entry of women into paid work, particularly in the South where employment rates are already at a very low level. When discussing trends and changes in women's roles, it is important to remember that the resulting transformations are plural, contingent and discontinuous and strongly shaped by prevailing socio-economic conditions. In the context of a prolonged and severe crisis, the differences between Northern and Southern Italy have been further accentuated, impeding the development of coherent policy responses and obstructing change in gender roles.

1. Introduction

Media coverage of the economic crisis in Italy has yielded striking representations of the position of women in the labour market. We will confine our attention to two sets of images which are particularly relevant. The first registers the importance of women's paid work, with all of the difficulties that accompany it. It includes the presence of women on picket lines and outside the gates of firms threatened with closure or redundancies. Often working in companies where women predominate, the militancy and determination of these women – often married with children – is striking:

> We are willing to take any kind of action – they will not manage to send us away. All the women are united and our families are behind us in this battle, which is not easy. Some of our husbands have been laid off, we have young children and mortgages to repay.[1]

A more traditional image of working women also persists, as wives and mothers who contribute to the family budget by earning a 'secondary' income. In a company near Milan, only women were exposed to redundancies, 'so that they can stay at home and look after the children', according to the owners: 'after all, what they bring home is only a second wage' (*Corriere della Sera* 2011). After unions intervened, the company was forced to revise its position.

The second set of images involves 'discouraged' women. The percentage of Italians falling into this category has risen during the crisis years, reaching 11.1% of the labour force in 2012, the highest rate in the European Union. These images capture the essence of the North-South divide in Italy, particularly as it relates to women. The first reflects the integration of women within the labour market, but mainly refers to the North of the country.[2] The second refers mainly to women in the South of Italy who are situated *outside* the labour market and may describe themselves as housewives, although in many cases they would like to have a paid job.

The tensions that characterise these two areas of Italy are quite different, although the role of women has changed in both macro-regions and the same demographic tensions are found, associated with low fertility

---

1. OMSA worker interviewed by Elisabetta Reguitti for *Articolo21* and accessed on 6 November 2011: http://www.articolo21.org/604/notizia/omsa-al-via-le-deloca lizzazioni-ma-le.html.
2. Throughout this article we will use the terms 'North' and 'South' to describe the two macro-areas of Italy. In the former we include the regions of the Centre, as these are more similar to the North than to the South, at least as far as women's roles are concerned. The North includes the following Regions: Valle d'Aosta, Piedmont, Liguria, Lombardy, Veneto, Trentino Alto Adige, Friuli Venezia Giulia, Emilia Romagna, Tuscany, Marche, Umbria, Lazio, Abruzzo. All other Regions are included in the South.

rates and population ageing. In what follows, we will question Esping-Andersen's account of the 'incomplete revolution', arguing that recent transformations in the role of women have given rise to plural, contingent and discontinuous outcomes which are not converging towards a single model. On the contrary, these changes must be understood in relation to the specific national and regional contexts in which they occur.

The article is divided into four sections: in the first, we briefly review Esping-Andersen's contribution (2009) to the debate about social change in Europe; in the second, we discuss the integration of women within the Italian labour force; in the third, we outline the contradictions that are emerging in social inequalities and care arrangements in the North and South, with a focus on collective early childcare services and transfer payments for care of the elderly and disabled; in the final section, we assess the impact of the ongoing economic crisis on the situation of women in Italy.

2. The social impact of changes in the role of women

Most commentators are in agreement that the massive entry of women into paid employment represents one of the most significant social transformations in post-war Europe (Goldin 2006; Esping-Andersen 2009). Rising levels of female employment are widely considered to be an important component of economic development, boosting demand, improving the efficiency of investment in education and training and encouraging economic innovation. Esping-Andersen (2009) observes:

> *The quiet revolution of women's roles, as Claudia Goldin (2006) calls it, is arguably a close rival to new technologies in terms of its seismic aftershocks touching, directly and indirectly, all major social institutions. And, like its rivals, it has not yet come to full maturation. Incomplete revolutions tend to be associated with major disequilibria.* (Esping-Andersen 2009: 1)

Esping-Andersen's description of this transformation stresses its profound effects on individual behaviour in relation to education, marriage, family life and parenting. His main argument is that the 'revolution' in gender roles has not yet been accomplished, provoking profound social tensions. The previous 'equilibrium' – based on the adult male 'breadwinner' model and a rigid gender division of labour inside and outside the home – has been swept away, but has not (yet) been replaced by a new balance (Esping-Andersen 2009: 10). We are therefore caught in a state of instability between competing models:

This occurs primarily because the revolution is spearheaded by women from the privileged social classes, the highly educated. It is only when it starts to seriously trickle down to the lower social strata, that the revolution enters a state of maturity that, in turn, is a precondition for more egalitarian outcomes. Put bluntly, the quest for gender equality tends to produce social inequality as long as it is a middle-class affair. (Esping Andersen 2009: 169)

Tensions are inevitable across various domains, manifesting themselves in low fertility rates, fertility postponement, increasing inequalities and social polarisation (Esping-Andersen 2009: 25, 86). Esping-Andersen stresses the important role of public policies in supporting gender equality, situating these in relation to family structures and the market, in line with his earlier work on welfare regimes (Esping-Andersen 1990). He focuses on two fields in particular – early childcare services and services for elderly people who are no longer self-sufficient – to emphasise the important role of public policies in fostering a new gender balance.

Citing the United States and Scandinavia – the most advanced countries in relation to gender equality – he suggests that they might serve 'as ideal typical images of what is crystallizing throughout the advanced world' (Esping-Andersen 2009: 173). He is convinced that other countries will follow, including Southern Europe, where the transformation in women's roles is occurring 'at an astonishing pace'. In Spain, he observes, the female employment rate has increased by 65% since 1990. Focusing on younger women with children, he observes that 'female employment is now close to US rates' (Esping-Andersen 2009: 7):

In fact, we must conclude that the portrait of Spanish family life as the epitome of traditionalism no longer holds. Young parents behave increasingly like Americans when it comes to who reads with the children or washes the dishes. (Esping-Andersen 2009: 173)

Italy is one of Esping-Andersen's 'laggard' countries, with one of the lowest female employment rates in Europe (47.5% for those aged 15–64 years in mid 2012) and a very high female inactivity rate (46.3%).[3] Italy scores very poorly in terms of the presence of women in the highest occupational groups and they systematically earn less than men, controlling for occupation (Istat 2010a). Italian women tend to withdraw from the labour market after the birth of their first or (particularly) second child. Italy also has a very low fertility rate and a

---

3. Labour force data published by the National Institute of Statistics, downloaded from the website http://dati.istat.it.

disproportionately high dependency rate, yielding an anomalous set of values for these key indicators.

The reason for the anomaly is that these indicators average across very different regional situations. We argue that the 'incomplete revolution' – and the transformations that accompany this – is occurring at a different rate and giving rise to different tensions in different parts of Italy. The Italian case comprises two macro-regions with very different female employment rates, varying from just 32.1% in the South to 56.0% in the North, a differential of almost 25 percentage points (for women aged 15–64 years). These different rates coincide with great disparities in family arrangements and public policies, demonstrating that the 'incomplete revolution' is non-linear, plural and divergent.

We share Esping-Andersen's conviction that contemporary European societies are undergoing far-reaching change in relation to gender roles, and that this is largely driven by (but not limited to) rising levels of female employment (Esping-Andersen 2009: 215). A key insight is that changes in women's roles are occurring in unexpected places, even where female employment remains low. At the same time, we are not convinced by Esping-Andersen's assumption that the advanced capitalist countries are progressing at different speeds along the same path. Even if female employment has increased in all of these countries, the context in which this has occurred has shaped the social and institutional consequences of this transformation in a very substantial way.

3. The partial integration of Italian women within the labour market

The (re-)entry of women into paid work in Italy started later and progressed more slowly than the United States or Scandinavia. At the time of the 1971 Census, female employment had fallen to a historical low, one of the lowest levels observed anywhere in Western Europe (25% in the North and 17% in the South). The North of Italy was one of the most intensely industrialised areas of Europe, although the majority of married women with children were full-time housewives. Female employment in the South was still concentrated in agriculture, whilst the cities offered few employment opportunities for women.

During the first three decades following WWII, the North–South divide decreased, at least when measured in terms of income *per capita* (Daniele and Malanima 2007). This was due to strong economic growth at national level, incisive regional development policies and infrastructural investments, although outmigration from the South also played a role. The state-led industrialisation process was not, however, of sufficient intensity to permanently alter labour market dynamics in the South. By the 1980s, the economic differential between North and South was once again increasing. Whilst economic restructuring and a decline in outmigration was pushing the South towards a chronic employment crisis, the Centre-North was embarking upon an intensive process of 'new industrialisation'. As these distinct processes unfolded, two patterns of change in women's roles took shape, co-existing within a single national context (Figure 1).

The increase in female employment and labour force participation rates, after reaching a low in 1971, followed a complex trajectory, which can be divided into two periods. The first lasted from the mid 1970s to the early 1990s, when a severe economic crisis shook the country; the second began in the mid 1990s and continued until the onset of the current economic crisis.

During the first period, the increase in female activity rates was relatively contained in all regions of Italy – roughly 10 percentage points – with similar trends in the North and South. In the North, the increase was almost entirely due to the growth of female employment, whilst in the South, the supply of female labour fuelled an increase in unemployment.

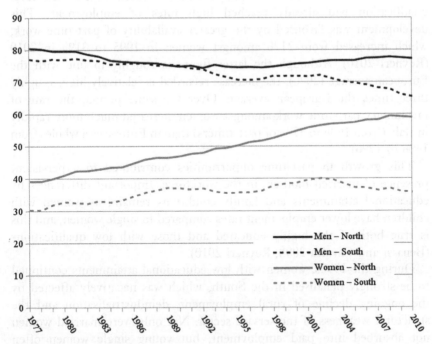

Figure 1. Labour force participation rate by gender and macro-region in Italy, 1977–2010
Source: Istat, *Rilevazione trimestrale* and *Rilevazione continua sulle forze di lavoro*, 1977–2010 (downloaded from: http://seriestoriche.istat.it/fileadmin/allegati/Mercato_del_lavoro/Tavole/Tavola_10.6.1.xlsx)

In 1978, the activity rates of women in the North and South differed by about 10 percentage points, rising to more than 15 in 1993. The differential in employment rates was even larger, rising from 13.2% in 1978 to 19.5% in 1993 (Pruna 2008). This increase in female labour force participation rates reflected the increasing importance of paid work to Italian women in general. The driving force behind this process was the rapid increase in educational attainments, which explains the great frustration of women in the South, who were often excluded from the labour market.

By the 1990s, the movement of married women into the permanent labour force in Northern Italy signalled a largely irreversible transition. This growth was mainly due to the expansion of dynamic sectors of the economy – ICTs, fashion, design and advanced producer services – and occurred against the backdrop of a very weak network of welfare services and an almost exclusive attribution of family responsibilities to women (Istat 2007: 18).

Employment growth in the North during the 1990s benefited women with relatively low educational attainments as women with a third-level qualification had already reached high rates of employment. This development was favoured by the greater availability of part-time work, which increased from 21% amongst women in 1995 to 31% in 2010 (Reyneri 2010). Although the latter figure is roughly in line with the European average (29%), the increase recorded is relatively high, roughly three times the European average. Over the same period, the rate of involuntary part-time work amongst women increased much more rapidly in Italy (from 16% to 37% of part-timers) than in Europe as a whole (from 14% to 17%).[4]

This growth in part-time opportunities contributed to a persistent presence of married mothers in the workforce. Important differences by educational attainments and family conditions remain, as women with children have lower employment rates compared to single women, and this is true both of the highly educated and those with low qualifications. (Benassi and Cavalca 2008; Reyneri 2010).

During the 1990s, women with low educational attainments continued to be strongly penalised in the South, which was negatively affected by the ongoing decline of rural employment, deindustrialisation and the structural weakness of the service sector. Not only were married women not absorbed into paid employment, but young single women often remained outside the labour market. The female unemployment rate reached particularly high levels in the South during the 1980s (rising from

---

4. OECD data accessed on 3 March 2012 from http://stats.oecd.org/Index.aspx.

18.2% in 1980 to 31.0% in 1988), decreasing during the early 1990s only to increase once again over the following decade.[5]

Starting in the New Millenium, however, the female unemployment rate in the South declined considerably, levelling off at 15% in 2008. This was due to the growth of female employment from a low base as well as 'discouragement' effects. The difficulties involved in finding a relatively stable, regular job for young women continue to suffocate female activity rates in the South. As a result, where young, highly qualified women find stable employment, they tend to remain at work. This is partly due to the prevalence of public sector employment, which also provides a greater opportunity to reconcile paid work and domestic/care responsibilities.

As a result of these trends, a polarisation in life chances has occurred in the South between highly educated women and those with lower qualifications, who are mainly forced into the role of housewife. When in paid employment, less qualified women often work in low-paid service jobs with very long hours and low incomes (Villa 2010; Andreotti and Fellini 2012).

The sluggish rate of employment growth observed in the South means that women have generally not been drawn into the labour force, despite their increasing aspirations, rising education levels and positive attitudes towards paid work, to which we will return below. This constitutes a key aspect of the contradictory modernisation of women's work in Italy, and reflects the persistence of a profound territorial dualism unique among European countries.

As we have shown, there are qualitatively distinct forms of integration within the labour market in the North and South of Italy. Despite their differences, it is possible to identify aspects of 'modernisation' in both areas, driven by an increase in female educational participation. Women aged 15–19 years have a high rate of attendance at secondary school (approximately 80%) and (as in other European countries) tend to have higher attainments. There is still a gap between North and South in relation to third-level education, as the percentage of women aged 30–34 with a third-level degree in the South (18.9%) is almost 10 points below the equivalent figure in the North (27.1%; Istat 2010a).

---

5. Data published by the National Institute of Statistics and downloaded in March 2012 from the website http://seriestoriche.istat.it/fileadmin/allegati/Mercato_del_lavoro/ Tavole/Tavola_10.8.1.xls. Data collection procedures and definitions were modified by the National Institute of Statistics in 1992 and 2003, which creates interruptions in the data series. A sharp drop is evident in the official estimate of the female unemployment rate in the South between 1992 (28.6%) and 1993 (20.0%), which should be borne in mind when analysing Figure 1.

As far as family formation and children are concerned, a process of convergence is evident, with a fertility rate in the South of 1.35 (1.43 in the North), and an age of 30.6 years at birth of first child, compared to 31.6 in the North. In both areas, it is quite common for children to live with their parents into adulthood and to delay leaving the family home (29–30 years) (Billari *et al.* 2008). The divorce rate (per 10,000 residents) is relatively low in both areas (11.9 in the South and 15.5 in the North), although the marriage rate (per 1000 residents) is somewhat higher in the South (4.6, compared to 3.7 in the North).[6]

Attitudinal data confirm this overall picture of convergence in attitudes and expectations. The last European Value Survey reveals only small differences between Northern and Southern Italian women regarding attitudes towards paid work: 91% of women in the South consider work important, as against 96% in the North. Similarly, 69% of women living in the South, in central age cohorts, agree with the phrase 'people get lazy if they are not working' (the equivalent figure is 67% in the North). Even more significantly, 17% of young adult women in the South strongly agree with the phrase 'work always comes first', while in the North the equivalent figure is just 8%.

This clearly reflects the importance that women attach to paid employment, and testifies to the fact that women in both the North and South desire to work and could be mobilised to enter the labour market, which would yield considerable social and economic benefits (Ferrera 2008; Naldini and Saraceno 2011; Del Boca *et al.* 2012).

Labour market differences between North and South form part of the diversified picture of social change, welfare provision and social inequality in contemporary Italy. In the South, there are high levels of unemployment and poverty and relatively low levels of regular employment, whilst welfare systems are starved of resources. The combined result is a vicious cycle based on the inter-generational transmission of social inequalities that penalises young people and children. We will explore this issue in the next section, before discussing the tensions that are emerging in relation to early childcare services and care for the elderly and disabled.

4. Local welfare systems

The Italian Regions are highly polarised in terms of poverty, having some of the highest and lowest rates in Europe. In the South, the poverty rate was 23% in 2010, whilst the equivalent rate in the North was just 5.3%.

6. All data were published by the National Institute of Statistics and downloaded in March 2012 from the website: http://noi-italia.istat.it.

This differential becomes even more dramatic when we consider the proportion of children living in poverty. Comparative data for OECD countries indicate that the child poverty rate in the South of Italy is twice the national average of 15% (compared to a European average of 12.4%), and almost half of all families with three or more children (47.3%) fall into this category. This is the result of various factors, including the uneven distribution of unemployment risks, precarious jobs and the number of families with just one wage-earner (Barbieri *et al.* 2012).[7]

Within this dualistic context, welfare policies are largely ineffective in reducing the risk of poverty. If we consider child poverty rates before and after social transfers, the Italian differential is just 7 percentage points, compared to an average of 14 points for the EU-27 (Istat 2010a). It is not difficult to imagine that this average conceals large regional differences; given that average per capita spending on social welfare is just 52 Euro in the Southern Regions, less than half the national average of 111.[8]

In order to understand how these socio-economic factors interact with family structure and public policies, we will provide examples relating to two crucial areas of welfare provision: early childcare and subsidies for care of elderly and disabled people who are not able to look after themselves.

Collective early childcare services have been identified as a crucial factor both in tackling the effects of child poverty (Gunnarsson *et al.* 1999; Esping-Andersen 2009; Morel *et al.* 2011) and in sustaining female employment, with a positive impact on women with low formal qualifications (Saraceno 2003; OECD 2007; Del Boca *et al.* 2008; Ferrera 2008). This is precisely what the South needs, as it would contribute to breaking the 'vicious cycle' of low female participation rates, high poverty rates and weak welfare services. Unfortunately, the large-scale development of early childcare services is unlikely to obtain the necessary political support, given the present social and economic conditions. Collective childcare services for children aged 0–2 years are scarce throughout Italy and the Barcelona target has not yet been reached in almost any Region.[9] The situation is particularly dramatic in the South, where only one-third (35.7%) of Municipalities have at least one

---

7. Italy has the lowest percentage of all EU member states for dual-income families, according to EU SILC data for 2007 (58.4%, compared to a European average of 76.1% (Istat 2010b).
8. Data published by the National Institute of Statistics and downloaded in March 2012 from the website: http://noi-italia.istat.it.
9. The Italian coverage rate for services targeted at children between three and five years is, by contrast, almost universal across the country.

collective early childcare service, compared with 65.8% in the North, and only 4.3% of children attend public childcare (15.1% in the North; Istat 2010a).

The South therefore remains trapped within a vicious cycle in which low labour force participation rates among women reduce the demand for welfare services and the low availability of these services penalises low-income families and reduces the demand for female employees. Those women who manage to find a job cannot rely on public services when seeking to reconcile these roles. The prevailing forms of work-family balance in the South are driven by the requirements of women with high educational attainments and high incomes, who have the highest employment rates and often the most favourable working conditions in terms of flexibility and parental leave.

The exclusion of low-qualified women from the labour market and the restriction of employment opportunities primarily to the well-educated contribute to increasing social inequalities. The indirect effect – which is crucial – is to undermine political pressure for the extension of the welfare state, impeding a new gender balance. The political system in the South is itself characterised by a conservative approach to welfare policies, which receive little public attention.

The employment crisis and cuts in public spending on services is making it more difficult to identify anything resembling a new 'gender-equality equilibrium' (Esping-Andersen 2009: 11). By contrast, the 'familistic' character of the gender division of labour in Southern Italy reinforces a vicious cycle that has impeded a shift from the family to collective provision of care, depressing demand and preventing the expansion of female employment.

In the North of Italy, where women in the central age cohorts are generally at work, a partial and selective process of defamilisation has taken place. Defamilisation here is predicated on an articulated set of arrangements, including a complex division of domestic labour comprising an inter-generational 'pact' and an expansion of paid domestic labour, primarily involving immigrant women. More than half (55%) of working women with children under two years in the North rely regularly on their own parents or parents-in-law for informal childcare, whilst one quarter use a public (15%) or private nursery (12%) and 11% rely on a child-minder (Istat 2005).[10] These intergenerational links – which are often

---

10. In Denmark, a high percentage of families (60%) also look to grandparents to help with childcare. However, the intensity of involvement is very different, with grandparents in Denmark contributing an average of seven hours per week, compared with no less than 27.8 hours per week in Italy – almost the equivalent of a full-time job (Esping Andersen 2009).

cemented by residential patterns (more than one quarter of adults live in the same Municipality as their parents) – enable low-paid women to remain within the labour market, even in the absence of effective public services.

In this context, it is evident that having access to grandparents becomes a powerful source of inequalities (Andreotti et al. 2005). Immigrant families, those from other regions and those whose own parents are still at work encounter greater difficulties in organising childcare.[11] This effect is likely to become more pronounced in the future due to greater geographical mobility and recent increases in the retirement age.

Working mothers in the North face particular difficulties in reconciling work and family responsibilities, and a key challenge is to find a way of remaining within the labour market without creating gendered occupational 'ghettos' (Del Boca and Saraceno 2005; Naldini and Saraceno 2011). This marks a fundamental difference in relation to the South, as women in the Mezzogiorno have generally not obtained the extended social role underlying this dilemma. The main tensions found in this macro-region, by contrast, relate to the reproduction of inequalities and poverty. At the same time, women who do have this dual role in the South and have low qualifications face even greater difficulties than their Northern counterparts because they are forced to rely on a network of public services which is weaker and frequently of a lower quality.

The example of early childcare services highlights the different tensions in the two macro-areas in relation to the role of women and the demand for welfare. The next example reveals the differential impacts of specific policy measures and relates to the non-self-sufficient elderly. Collective services for people who are not self-sufficient are weak, costly and unevenly distributed in Italy. The principal policy measure is a monetary transfer: the Indennità di accompagnamento. This payment is provided on grounds of certified invalidity and is not means-tested. In 2007, 11.9% of elderly people received this payment, with a particularly high take-up rate in the South (Naldini and Saraceno 2011).

This subsidy has encouraged female employment in the North by enabling women to keep their jobs even in the presence of care burdens, whilst subsidising immigrant caregivers, who have been attracted to this part of Italy. It has been possible for women to delegate care in this

11. In this regard, it is interesting to note that the Minister for the Family in Germany, Kristina Schröder, recently proposed a 'Family Time' scheme whereby grandparents would have the right to leave from work in order to assist with caring for young children (Corriere della Sera 2012).

way, maintaining overall responsibility for family members, because of the cheap wages and irregular status of many of the female immigrants who take up these jobs. In this context, an apparently neutral policy measure has a series of positive but unintended consequences for female employment.

In the South, by contrast, it is much more common for a female relative to take on a direct caring role. As alternative employment opportunities are scarce, care-givers frequently use the transfer payment as income. Transfer payments for care of the elderly and disabled thus create a further disincentive to female employment, reinforcing family responsibilities and the vicious cycle of low employment, poverty and depressed demand for welfare services. Due to the great social differences between North and South, therefore, it is quite possible for a single policy measure to yield diametrically opposed outcomes.

5. Impact of the crisis and the prospects of the 'incomplete revolution' in Italy

During its initial stages, the economic crisis had a disproportionate impact on male employment, due to its effect on traditionally 'male' sectors such as construction and manufacturing. As it has progressed, however, the crisis has effectively interrupted the expansion of female employment. The unemployment rate has risen rapidly over the past 4 years (by roughly 3 percentage points throughout Italy) reaching almost 20% in the South by mid 2012 (for those aged 15–64). Although the male rate has risen even more rapidly (by 4 percentage points in the North and by more than 6 points in the South), the gender gap in unemployment in Italy remains one of the highest in Europe. Interestingly, the *female* employment rate in the North is now higher than the *male* rate in the South for individuals aged 25–34 years.[12]

Older women have been somewhat less penalised by the crisis than younger women, due primarily to its effects on job creation. There has been a dramatic reduction in short-term contracts, where younger workers predominate (IRES 2010; Istat 2010a).[13] In Italy as a whole, the rate of temporary employment contracts amongst women increased from 11% in 2000 to 15% in 2007, dropping back to

---

12. Quarterly data from the *Rilevazione continua sulle forze di lavoro* published by the National Institute of Statistics, downloaded in October 2012 from the website http://dati.istat.it.

13. If we consider overall employment in Italy between 2008 and 2010, semi-autonomous positions (*collaborazioni*) declined by 15%, whilst temporary contracts fell by almost 5% in the North and 8% in the South. Qualified women in the South have a particularly high rate of atypical contracts (Avola 2009; Istat 2011).

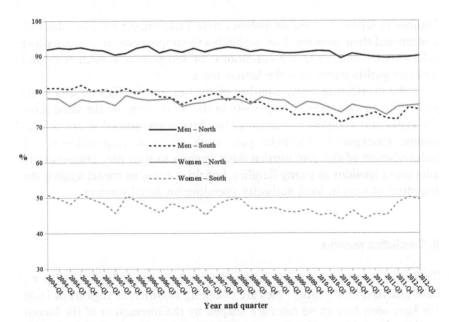

Figure 2. Age-specific (25–34 years) participation rate by macro-region and gender, 2004–2011
Source: *Rilevazione continua sulle forze di lavoro*, quarterly data downloaded from http://dati.istat.it.

13% in 2010.[14] The latter decline was not due to an expansion of permanent jobs but rather to the more rapid contraction of temporary employment. Young people in Italy are increasingly either in precarious jobs or outside the labour force (Figure 2). Even young women with a third-level education in the South have been hit by the crisis, while those with lower qualifications are more discouraged.

We have already hinted at the most likely effects of these trends in the immediate future: a further increase in unemployment, particularly amongst young men and women in the South and an increase in outmigration, particularly amongst the highly educated (cf. Mocetti and Porello 2010). The fact that a growing number of female graduates are forced to leave the country in search of jobs further undermines the link between educational attainments and female emancipation.

In the South, the crisis is likely to be particularly intense and selective in its effects. The incidence of poverty is destined to increase, particularly amongst large and single-earner families. The number of dual-income

14. A similar trend was observed for OECD countries in general, with an initial rise from 9.9% in 2000 to 11.1% in 2007, followed by a decline, to reach 10.8% in 2010 (Comparable OECD data downloaded from http://stats.oecd.org/Index.aspx, 3 March 2012).

families is falling and public policies have little impact on low-educated women and their families. This highlights the importance of implementing reforms that can create the conditions for integrating women with and without qualifications into the labour force.

In the North, the larger number of dual-earner families affords some protection against the risk of poverty in the short-term. At the same time, the crisis and the policy measures that have accompanied it are undermining strategies to reconcile paid work and care responsibilities. A redistribution of the care burden from women to men may contribute to alleviating tensions in young families, but these tensions are set against the backdrop of cuts in local authority spending on social services.

6. Concluding remarks

Taking as our starting-point Esping-Andersen's recent book (2009), we have analysed how gender roles are changing in different regions of Italy. We have seen how these roles are shaped by the interaction of the labour market, the public welfare system and informal care arrangements, giving rise to different tensions. In the North, it is increasingly difficult to reconcile work and family roles, not least as a result of retrenchment. The fragile balance centred on the care work of grandparents and low-paid immigrant women is increasingly untenable. In the South, female participation and employment rates remain at an extremely low level, with far-reaching consequences in terms of child poverty and social inequalities. Apparently neutral policy measures can, in this context, give rise to very different outcomes, as we argued in relation to subsidies for care of the elderly and disabled.

Although there has been a sharp rise in educational attainments amongst young women, leading to a stronger orientation towards autonomy and positive attitudes towards paid work, gender roles in Italy do not appear to be converging towards a single model. Although the expansion in educational participation, the influence of the TV and other media have changed the cultural values and opinions of Northern and Southern women in similar ways, the lack of employment opportunities, the weakness of welfare and increasing inequalities in the South are pushing gender roles towards a highly unequal configuration.

The persistently large group of women excluded from regular forms of employment may be described as housewives, but increasingly perceive this condition as imposed and involuntary. Other women are pushed to emigrate or must accept lengthy commutes in order to find a job, whilst a third group struggles to get by with low-paid and unstable jobs and limited access to welfare services. We thus observe neither the 'conservative' defence of traditional gender roles nor an 'incomplete revolution' based on the gradual overcoming of gender inequalities.

The policies under discussion include incentives to firms which create new jobs for women and facilitate the entry of young people into paid employment. These policies may have a positive impact on young women in the North, but do not resolve tensions surrounding care arrangements for dependent family members. They are also unlikely to have an impact on the depressed labour market of the South, where women are discouraged from – but ready to – entering the labour market and male employment is in decline. This is due to the fact that there are few employment occasions, given the weak network of firms and because incentives cannot compete with informal and black market activities. The positive trends in female employment visible between 2000 and 2008 have been slowed down by the crisis and the reserves of labour in the South appear destined to remain under-utilised, excluding new patterns of economic development, even though a raise in female employment (central age cohorts) is visible in 2012.

In order to change this state of affairs, it is necessary to break the vicious cycle of social inequalities in the South of Italy. One of the most urgent tasks is to create employment opportunities for young people, particularly low-skilled young women. An employment policy of this type would be particularly effective if oriented towards the goal of developing welfare services, as this would trigger an extended transformation of women's roles in accordance with the model of the 'incomplete revolution'.

Arguably, overcoming the large employment gap that separates low-educated women in the North and South would contribute to pressure for welfare reform to reduce the care burden that is currently attributed to women. Effective paternity leave, accessible and high-quality childcare for pre-school children and a network of services for care of the elderly and disabled are obvious examples of what is required, but these demands are increasingly difficult to articulate, let alone to achieve, in a situation where only a minority of women have the opportunity to take up paid employment.

References

Andreotti, A. and Fellini, I. (2012) 'Dentro la crisi: partecipazione e occupazione femminili in un mercato del lavoro territorialmente diviso', *Sociologia del Lavoro* 126(2): 11–24.

Andreotti, A., Fraisse, L. and Sabatinelli, S. (2003) *Welfare Mix and Social Cohesion: Does the Diversification of Childcare Services Increase Social*

Cohesion? EMES Working Paper: http://www.emes.net/fileadmin/ emes/ PDF_files/Child_care_Transversal_Jun_04.pdf.

Barbieri, P., Cutuli G. and Tosi, M. (2012) 'Famiglie, mercato del lavoro e rischi sociali. Nascita di un figlio e rischi di transizione alla povertà tra le famiglie italiane', *Stato e Mercato* 3: 391–428.

Benassi, D. and Cavalca, G. (2008) 'Le donne come attori del mutamento sociale: I comportamenti occupazionali femminili in cinque aree urbane', *Sociologia del lavoro* 110: 83–98.

Billari, F. C., Rosina, A., Ranaldi, R. and Romano, M. C. (2008) 'Young Adults Living Apart and Together (LAT) with parents: A three-level analysis of the Italian case', *Regional Studies* 42(5): 625–39.

Corriere della Sera (2011) 'Azienda licenzia solo le donne: «Così stanno a casa con I figli»', Milan Edition, 30 June.

Corriere della Sera (2012) 'Il congedo «guarda nipoti» per i nonni che lavorano', 15 March.

Daniele, V. and Malanima, P. (2007) 'Il prodotto delle regioni e il divario Nord-Sud in Italia', *Rivista di politica economica* 97: 1–49.

Del Boca, D., Mencarini, L. and Pasqua, S. (2012) *Valorizzare le donne conviene*, Bologna: Il Mulino.

Del Boca, D., Pasqua, S. and Pronzato, C. (2008) *Market Work and Motherhood Decisions in Contexts*, IZA Discussion paper no. 3303.

Del Boca, D. and Saraceno, C. (2005) 'Le donne in Italia tra famiglia e lavoro', *Economia e lavoro* XXXIX(1): 125–40.

Esping Andersen, G. (2009) *The Incomplete Revolution*, Cambridge: Polity Press.

Esping Andersen, G. (1990) *The Three Worlds of Welfare Capitalism*, Cambridge: Polity Press.

Ferrera, M. (2008) *Perché il lavoro delle donne farà crescere l'Italia*, Milano: Mondadori.

Goldin, C. (2006) 'The quiet revolution that transformed women's employment education and family', *American Economic Review* 96: 1–21.

Gunnarsson, L., Martin Korpi, B. and Nordensram, U. (1999) *Early Childhood Education and Care Policy in Sweden, Background Report.* OECD Thematic review, Stockholm: Ministry of Education and Science.

IRES (2010) *Il lavoro atipico al tempo della crisi: dati e riflessioni sulle dinamiche recenti del mercato del lavoro, Rapporto IRES 5/2010*, Rome: IRES.

Istat (2005) *Indagine sulle nascite in Italia*, Rome: Istat.

Istat (2007) *I tempi della vita quotidiana Un approccio multidisciplinare all'analisi dell'uso del tempo*, Argomenti no. 32, Rome: Istat.

Istat (2010a) *Rapporto sull'Italia*, Rome: Poligrafica dello Stato.

Istat (2010b) 'Audizione dell'Istituto nazionale di statistica', d.ssa Linda Laura Sabbadini, Direttore, Direzione Centrale per le indagini su condizioni e qualità della vita presso la Commissione Permanente "Lavoro, previdenza sociale", Senato della Repubblica: http://www. istat.it/it/files/2011/01/allegato.pdf.

Mocetti, S. and Porello, C. (2010) 'La mobilità del lavoro in Italia: nuove evidenze sulle dinamiche migratorie', *Quaderni della Banca d'Italia* 61. http://www.bancaditalia.it/pubblicazioni/econo/quest_ecofin_2/QF_61.

Morel, N., Palier, B. and Palme, J. (eds) (2011) *Towards a Social Investment Welfare State? Ideas, Policies, Challenges,* Bristol: Policy Press.

Naldini, C. and Saraceno, C. (2011) *Conciliare famiglia e lavoro,* Bologna: Il Mulino.

OECD (2007) *Babies and Bosses: Reconciling Work and Family Life,* Paris: OECD.

Pruna, M. L. (2008) 'Donne del Nord, Donne del Sud. La dimensione territoriale delle disuguaglianze di genere nel mercato del lavoro', *Sociologia del lavoro* 110: 55–68.

Reyneri, E. (2010) 'Offerta di lavoro e occupazione femminile', in E. Reyneri (ed.), *Il lavoro delle donne,* Rome: CNEL, www.portalecnel.it

Saraceno, C. (2003) 'La conciliazione di responsabilità familiari e lavorative: paradossi ed equilibri imperfetti', *Polis* XVII(2): 199–228.

Villa, P. (2010) 'La crescita dell'occupazione femminile: la polarizzazione tra stabilità e precarietà', *Lavoro e diritto* XXIV(3): 343–58.

Index

Note:
Page numbers in **bold** type refer to figures
Page numbers in *italic* type refer to *tables*

Ancizu, I.: and Bazo, M.T. 98
Andreotti, A.: Mingione, E. and
  Pratschke, J. 19–20, 146–61
austerity 16, 132–42

bail outs 15, 16
Barometer of Sociological Research
  Centre 94
Bazo, M.T.: and Ancizu, I. 98
benefits: social 77
Bengtson, V.L.: and Roberts, E.L. 49
Bettio, F.: *et al* 47
Billingsley, S.: and Sarasa, S. 93, 101
Bonoli, G. 15
Brooks, C.: and Calzada, I. 18, 44–61

Cabrita, M.: Torres, A. and Coelho, B.
  18, 65–81
Caïs, J.: and Folguera, L. 19, 86–103
Calzada, I.: and Brooks, C. 18, 44–61
care: child 59–60, 155; dependence
  (Spain) 94–101; enrolment *38, 76*;
  family 35–40; gender 39; health 137–
  42; migrant-based model 106–22; needs
  112; preferences 45–7; public 55–60;
  responsibilities 72; social *138*; statutory
  services 141; support *37, see also* long-
  term care (LTC)
caring work: Spain demand 116
cash transfers 115
cash-for-care 111–13
Catholic Church 9, 25
Catholic marriage **68**, 80
Central Europe 29
child care: public 59–60, 155
child poverty: Southern Italy 155
childrearing: attitudes to *32*

children 154; born out of wedlock **69**;
  with parent unmarried and working
  fulltime *68*
CIS Barometer (Sept 2010) 94
Coelho, B.: Cabrita, M. and Torres, A.
  18, 65–81
cohabitation 28, *67*; attitudes to 31, *31*
Continental Europe: LTC 109
contracts: fixed-term 7
corruption scandals: Greece 135
cultural arrangements 18

Da Roit, B.: González Ferrer, A. and
  Moreno-Fuentes, F. 19, 106–22
Daatland, S.O.: and Lowenstein, A. 92
debt: crisis 127–31; public 1
democracy: liberal 53
dependence care: Spain 94–101
deprivation: severe 3–4
disability entitlement 34
distribution: outcomes 3–4
divorce: attitudes to *31*; rate **69**
domestic workers: foreign 116; registered
  in Spain *117*

economic crisis 14–16, 127, 146–61
economic restructuring 151
education: full-time completion **70**
employment: female *33*, 107, 110–21,
  110, 146–61; Greek conditions 141;
  Northern Italy growth 152; regime 7;
  Southern Italy growth 153; trajectories
  in Italy and Spain 106–22
envoi 4
Esping-Andersen, G. 45, 148, 149, 150
EU15: female activity rate *91*
EUROFAMCARE: National Background
  Report (2004) 93
European Monetary Union (EMU) 130

For Product Safety Concerns and Information please contact our
EU representative GPSR@taylorandfrancis.com Taylor & Francis
Verlag GmbH, Kaufingerstraße 24, 80331 München, Germany